ARCTIC MADNESS

Hau
Books

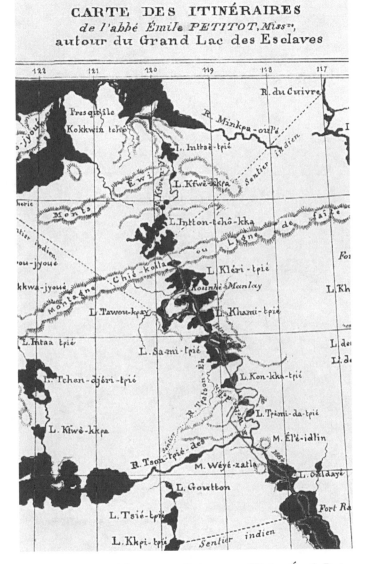

Frontispiece. Detail from map of itinerary of Father Émile Petitot, missionary, around Great Slave Lake. Émile Petitot, *Autour du Grand Lac des Esclaves* (Paris, A. Savine, 1891). © Zones sensibles, used with permission.

ARCTIC MADNESS

The Anthropology of a Delusion

Pierre Déléage

Translated by Catherine V. Howard

Hau Books
Chicago

Cover design: Daniele Meucci
Layout design: Deepak Sharma, Prepress Plus
Typesetting: Prepress Plus (www.prepressplus.in)

This book has received the support of the Laboratoire d'Excellence
(LABEX) TranferS.

ISBN: 978-1912808274
eBook: 978-1912808373
LCCN: 2020941277

Hau Books
Chicago Distribution Center
11030 S. Langley
Chicago, Il 60628
www.haubooks.com

Hau Books is printed, marketed, and distributed by The University
of Chicago Press.
www.press.uchicago.edu

Table of Contents

Illustrations

Images of snowflakes shown at the start of each section were drawn by Émile Petitot for his article, "Géographie de l'Athabaskaw-Mackenzie," *Bulletin de la Société de Géographie* 10 (1875): 279.

Figure 1. Father Émile Petitot at age thirty-six. Photograph taken in 1874, probably in Montreal, Canada, and used when he joined the Société de Géographie in 1875 in France. Photograph courtesy of Archives Deschâlets, Richelieu, Canada.

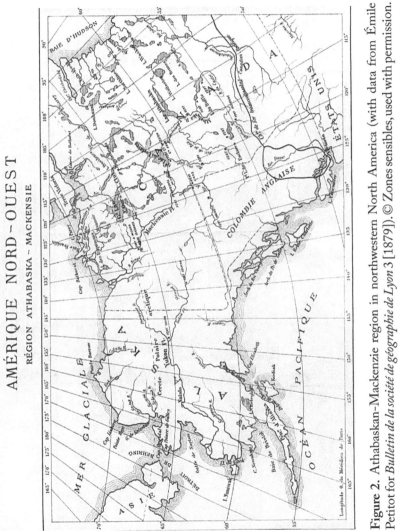

Figure 2. Athabaskan-Mackenzie region in northwestern North America (with data from Émile Petitot for *Bulletin de la société de géographie de Lyon 3* [1879]). © Zones sensibles, used with permission.

CHAPTER ONE

Persecution Mania
A Missionary among the First Nations

The Great Western and Erie Railroad train was pulling into Dunkirk, a small town in the westernmost part of New York State, where the train station was no more than a stone's throw from the southern shore of Lake Erie. Night had fallen a few hours ago, and lightning bolts sliced across the horizon at increasingly frequent intervals. Alone in a poorly lit section sat a balding, thirty-eight-year-old man with a top hat by his side, his attention divided between the spectacle of the storm and the pages of the book resting on his knees. Visible on the metal frame of his elegant glasses was an incision, chiseled by a Parisian engraver, that spelled the name of his protectress, Madame the Marquise de Vatimesnil, who would die twenty years later, one of numerous victims burned alive in a massive fire that struck the Charity Bazaar of Paris in 1897.[1] As the train came to a stop, the man put his book down next to his hat and looked out the window at the lively crowd in the station.

> At eight o'clock in the evening, an entire family of well-off artisans entered my train car and settled into a set of seats next to mine, leaving me by myself. I sprawled out on the velvet seats, one leg here, the other there, and enjoyed a cigar, adopting poses to make me look as much like a Yankee as possible.[2]

This traveler, a bit of a dandy, was on his way from New York City, where he had stayed at the home of a distant cousin to rest up after crossing the Atlantic. Returning to North America after a visit of almost two years in France, his native country, he was taking his time on the way back to where he had worked before his travel abroad. He knew how to savor long trips by train, with their intervals of half dozing, half reading and their unexpected events.

A girl about eighteen years old from this family did not hesitate to come to my section and take the corner seat facing me. Out of respect, I immediately assumed a less cavalier posture and threw my cigar out the transom window.

Since the train moving forward sent air and smoke into the face of my pretty neighbor, she asked if I would trade places with her, which I gladly deigned to do. In gratitude, my sweet neighbor launched right into conversation with me with charming ease and simplicity, all the while studying me from head to toe and back up again.[3]

Despite some discomfort, the man was not surprised by her manners, which would have seemed completely out of place in France. Although his work monopolized his attention and hardly gave him time to probe the young American's psychology, his twelve years on the continent had given him sufficient insight into the country's tradition of what he liked to call "the shocking overconfidence of the endearing sex." He felt it was only proper to offer his neighbor some of the dates, chocolate, and oranges he had brought along and then, under the dim light of the oil lamps, to engage in a bit of conversation before returning to his book.

After a quarter of an hour, she stood up and leaned over the back of her seat to talk to her mother sitting right behind her and let her know in a soft voice, "Mother, he's a gentleman. He's very refined." (This was more than flattering.) "He must be rich—he has a top hat and a big gold chain for his pocket watch. I think he's wonderful!"

This was said in a way to ensure I would hear everything. This saved her from having to make a declaration of love.[4]

Despite the apparent levity of his tone, the traveler, more surprised than shocked, felt a growing unease. He let himself discreetly contemplate the girl's features, mentally sketching one of those conventional portraits in the outdated academic style commonly used to depict the advent of spring. She caught his reticent, persistent gaze two or three times and seized each opportunity to stare back at him, immediately making him avert his eyes. These silent exchanges distracted the traveler from his reading. Upon reflection, he realized that a detail of this absurd situation dismayed him more than anything else, a detail that would not escape a clockmaker's son: the naïve creature sitting across from him had no idea about the value of watch chains, his having been bought for a mere ten francs on the modest Boulevard Poissonnière.

Soon the impressionable American sat down again and returned to her conversation. Note that she earnestly took me to be one of her fellow citizens.

"Where are you going to?" she asked me.

"To Saint Paul, in the state of Minnesota," I replied.

"Is that really far?"

"Not too far. Aren't you familiar with your country?"

"I don't have enough education for that. I'm a poor Irish girl."

"Catholic?"

"Oh, my Lord, no! I'm a Methodist and born in America."

"Ah, all right."

"And I should tell you, Sir, that I don't care for any creed, d'you see? But tell me," she continued, "where is that, Saint Paul? Is it farther than Sandusky?"

"Sandusky, you say? Sandusky? Who on earth knows where Sandusky is?!"

She grimaced in horror. "Sandusky? That's the city where we live!" she retorted. "What, you don't know about Sandusky?"

"Not a bit. . . . I swear this is the first time I've ever heard of it."

"Well, you absolutely must get to know Sandusky. You must come along with us! Oh, you will come, won't you?"[5]

The girl, hands clasped, adopted a pleading tone, and the traveler was momentarily struck dumb, seeking to regain his composure. He was troubled by her childlike frankness, her relaxed manners, her nonchalant atheism, her naïve certainty of occupying the center of the world.

I smiled sadly without answering but shook my head no. I didn't want the sweet child to notice that my emotions were beginning to well up, so I just kept quiet.

She became disconcerted, her mouth forming a charming little pout. While I pretended to watch the countryside in the moonlight, the weather having cleared up, I could see she was studying my face and trying to read my thoughts.

However, as we approached Cleveland. . . . her delicate Romanesque head understood that she had to hurry if she wanted to succeed.

"You're getting off in Cleveland, aren't you, Sir?" she inquired.

"No, Miss". . . .

"But we have to get off here to change to the train going to Sandusky. Oh, listen, you absolutely must come to Sandusky, it's pretty, so very pretty!"

"I'm very sorry, Miss, but I can't."

"What? You have a tour ticket. That gives you three months to travel wherever you want. You can stop anywhere you like. Don't deny it, I saw your ticket when the conductor punched it."

"Yes, but unfortunately I won't be getting off the train until I reach my destination."

"At your destination? Well, then, what are you, Sir, an officer?"

"No, Miss, I'm a Catholic priest," I replied, dropping the bomb to put an end to this sickening melodrama.[6]

On April 12, 1876, Émile Fortuné Stanislas Joseph Petitot, the addled traveler on the Great Western and Erie train, began the journey that was to bring him back to Our Lady of Good Hope Mission, just below the polar circle, where his beard would grow back and he would once again don his ecclesiastical attire. His fleeting encounter with the girl— who immediately left to rejoin her family after discovering he was nothing but a common priest—made such an impression on his emotions and imagination that, a decade later, he was able to recount it in detail in the first volume of his *Mémoires d'un missionaire*.[7] For a brief interval, he had been taken for a Yankee, a gentleman, and an eligible bachelor. A priest though he was, he let himself be charmed and, while flirting between Dunkirk and Cleveland, enjoyed embracing a new identity. Languidly reflecting on his mixed desires, he took the opportunity to fantasize about a parallel life.

★

As briefly as possible, to get it out of the way, let me summarize Émile Petitot's early life. He was born in 1838 and grew up in the city of Marseilles. His family moved often, since his father, a clockmaker, went from job to job in different shops at a steady pace. He was educated at a Catholic school on Rue Saint-Savournin, an institution that taught young people "whose place was in between the aristocracy and the lower classes and who went into administration, the arts, commerce, finance, industry, and the affluent professions."[8] He was fascinated by books he read by Arctic explorers and, most likely, by the *Annales de la propagation de la foi* (Annals of the Propagation of the Faith), a periodical that twice a month published accounts of the glorious sufferings of new martyrs whose adventures took them to the frontiers of Christendom. When he was seventeen, his father died, whereupon he discovered his calling as a missionary. He became a novice at the congregation of the Missionary Oblates of Mary Immaculate. Upon being ordained as a priest, he boarded the Norwegian, a ship sailing to Canada, where he would work for twelve years, from 1862 to 1874. He spent most of this time around the mission situated at Fort Good Hope on the banks of the Mackenzie River, which had its source in the Great Slave Lake and flowed into the Arctic Ocean. During the many years he spent there, he successfully improvised as a cartographer, linguist, ethnographer, and folklorist. He returned to France for two years, mainly in Paris, where he was fêted by the ultramontane bourgeoisie and aristocracy. He then went back to the missions in the Far North for another six years, from 1876 to 1882, which ended when he was locked up in an "insane asylum" in Montreal. After thirteen months of confinement, he was repatriated across the Atlantic, where he was relieved of his vows. Living in nostalgic, bitter solitude at the parish of Mareuil-lès-Meaux, he wrote seven volumes of his memoirs and several other works. He died in 1916.[9]

At the mission at Fort Good Hope, it was dark all winter, and temperatures in January almost never went above −22 degrees Fahrenheit. Émile Petitot became the missionary to a First Nations people called Peaux-de-Lièvre by the French (and, by the English, Hareskins), while his mission partner Jean Séguin dedicated himself to the evangelization of a group they called the Loucheux or Dindjié (whom the English called Kutchin).[10] These First

Nations belong to the broad Dené (Northern Athapaskan) language family and are southern neighbors of the Inuit. During Émile Petitot's time, they were nomadic hunters whose lives were governed by the alternation of the seasons. They dispersed in small bands during the winter and then gathered in larger groups during the summer for big-game hunting and collective ceremonies. From the end of the eighteenth century to the first half of the nineteenth, their traditional way of life had gradually adapted to the presence of permanent trade posts run by Hudson's Bay Company. They became accustomed to stopping there twice a year, after the winter and summer hunts, for several weeks. They exchanged fur pelts for Western goods, such as guns, metal containers, tobacco, flour, clothing, and alcohol, at set rates that were systematically unfavorable to them. A few of them settled near Fort Good Hope and sometimes frequented the mission of Our Lady of Good Hope (Notre Dame de Bonne Espérance), where Jean Séguin and Émile Petitot were waiting for them, anxious about the salvation of their infidel souls and always happy to acquire some new provisions through bartering.

★

The first time Émile Petitot saw the Dené, he could not suppress his repulsion. Through many years of reading of adventure novels and evangelistic propaganda, he had formed a fairly precise image of Native North Americans, commonly called "Indians" at the time. He thought he knew their customs, skills, appearance, and way of life. The encounter disappointed all his expectations:

> A horde, dressed in leather and exceptionally stinking, was camped at Frog Portage. At first glance, I was surprised by the peculiar appearance of their features. Their head is small, conical, and narrow; their chin, jutting forward, is so sharp that it looks ridiculous,

taking on the appearance of a fox or weasel. But their demeanor is serious, reserved, and honest, almost morose. Their eyes, very close to the bridge of their nose, which is large and aquiline, express an anxiety that grips them. Their mouth is subdued and relaxed. No outcries, no expansiveness, no enthusiasm whatsoever. They stand in line single file, take off their caps as if in a procession, and silently, with devotion or the hint of a serious smile, present their hands to you calmly after wiping them off on their clothes. One would think they were monks.[11]

If the physiognomy and appearance of the Dené peoples caused him, at least initially, an irrepressible aversion, their mores, which he gradually learned about and came to understand as the months went by, disconcerted him even more:

When I would get ready for bed, I was always surrounded by half a dozen patient witnesses who, after having emptied my cauldron and licked all my plates, watched the ceremony like the courtiers of Louis XIV did when he took a nap. Once they had left, dismissed with a gesture, and darkness began to spread, I heard mysterious whispers outside the house and saw three or four heads of laughing girls watching me indiscreetly.[12]

There was thus no privacy, even in the priests' house, which also served for a long time as a half-improvised confessional until a church was built and consecrated. The flocks of young women engaged in such spying not simply out of curiosity but also out of genuine lust for this twenty-five-year-old bachelor, who was well shaped, well dressed, and well respected by the White people (called the "bourgeois") of the Hudson's Bay Company, bearing an exotic aura and having a large stock of goods. His still youthful face, with its prominent angles, was surrounded by fair, fine hair set high on his forehead and by a beard that was both bushy and wispy, allowing a glimpse of a slightly bent, lean but muscular neck, engulfed in the buttoned collar of a black velvet blouse upon which a figure of Christ on an oversized cross merrily swung. His highly mobile mouth, stretched wide between its corners, would speak with a melodious accent. It was balanced by his light blue eyes, which were repeated by a pair of glasses with ovoid lenses that he never put aside, being as essential to him as his rosary. Easily chilled, he hardly ever, even at bedtime, took off his gloves or priest habit, which, during snowshoeing expeditions, he covered with trousers and coats made of animal skins, adding fur mittens, shoes, and hat to complete his outfit.

> One can well imagine that the detailed examination of my person gave rise to curious reflections. I saw myself transformed into an Adonis or Antinous by all the women and daughters present, who did not hesitate to say so out loud.[13]

The Catholic missionary, having become a Greek god, nourished this generalized lustfulness through his equivocal behavior.

> I have no doubt that I have been providing the women and girls many occasions to believe that I am courting them. It was by speaking kindly to them, smiling at them, and joking frankly with them, just like I did with the men, and especially by offering them food when they caught me eating my meals. "Among the redskins," said an English traveler whose name I forget, "looking at a woman, smiling at her, offering her a bite to eat or especially tobacco is considered a direct overture, which everyone understands without further explanation." This is absolutely true. Smiles were exchanged and bites of food were accepted as proof of acquiescence.

That was something I didn't understand then. When they eventually saw I was devoid of malice, the men informed me with a laugh that, unbeknownst to me, I used to represent a danger to their wives and daughters. "You are a libertine without even realizing it," they told me.[14]

The libertine's unself-conscious naïveté quickly evaporated. The advances made by the Indigenous women far surpassed the modest ones made by young women in the United States.

> Several times, a beautiful twenty-year-old girl came into my bedroom, sighing and gazing at me with a languid look.
>
> "What is it, Watpantsaze? You look like you're suffering, my child."
>
> "Your child? You're as young as I! Don't you see I'm suffering over you? Would you like me to wait for you in the woods?"

The women obviously did not play coy.[15]

Despite his comic portrayal of his confusion, one may wonder what it meant years later for the tired fifty-year-old, back in France, when he published this reminiscence as a minor priest in eastern Brie, Champagne. He was prematurely aged, bitter, and lost in memories of a distant land, recalling only seductions, misunderstandings, and vanities. Notwithstanding his half-admitted pose as a libertine priest, neither American nor First Nations women were genuine temptations for Émile Petitot. On the contrary, they inspired only distaste in him. In a letter to a superior, he confessed in peculiar terms that "the sight of the fair sex" was for him "like that of an ash tree or bamboo."[16] Neither vixens nor minks, female humans were merely part of the vegetable kingdom for him. The young priest was not attracted to women.

★

Despite the repugnance he expressed, celibacy weighed heavily on Émile Petitot, since young men did not leave him indifferent. He liked to use Indigenous or Métis subjects for his drawings. In his memoirs, he described with obvious pleasure an almost lascivious portrait of a youth named Dzanyu:

> This one is a handsome Dené, an Adonis among his compatriots, who are not especially handsome. He has intelligent, gentle, large black eyes that are shaded by long eyelashes, a strong and elevated brow, a straight nose flattened in the middle, a disdainfully curved lip, and a high but narrow forehead. However, this happy physiognomy was sometimes illuminated by peculiar flashes of guile. His gaze, ordinarily jovial and friendly, would become treacherous. His neck, stretched forward, would suggest something abhorrent, and his narrow temples would tense with obduracy. At those moments, something devilish, I don't know what, lurked inside this angelic Indian figure. I consider him, physically and morally, to be an excellent specimen of a Danite youth in the Far North.[17]

But the Dené youths would only pass briefly through the mission of Our Lady of Good Hope. They would suddenly appear as if out of nowhere, smiling and talkative, and then disappear just as suddenly, leaving the fort to go on an expedition, drawn to a trekking band in which they spotted a girl to their liking or eager to prove their hunting skills through exploits in remote areas. Émile Petitot suffered acute pangs over these departures:

> I could not get used to these frequent separations, the trips that made these nomadic beings so happy. What a joy for them to go back to live in the open air, to exchange

the dull chimney corner and floor for the elkskin lodge, with green branches scattered on the frozen ground and a large fire of blazing pine logs in the middle of the dwelling. They followed the reindeer as they wandered; they nourished themselves on the slaughter; they made eight, ten, twenty meals a day, if they so wished; they cut down patches of forest for firewood to warm themselves; and they enjoyed complete freedom without any outside interference.[18]

The missionary identified himself completely with the Dené youths, accompanying them in his thoughts, dreaming of what it would be like to cultivate male camaraderie far from the Church and its commandments. Nonetheless, he was required to stay at the mission, a few kilometers from the Hudson's Bay Company fort. The mission had four log cabins topped by gable roofs with chimneys that continuously spewed smoke. The cabins surrounded a church that Émile Petitot decorated to distract himself, its bell tower facing the river where boats of Indigenous and Métis travelers came and went, greeted by an immense wooden crucifix. Émile Petitot lived there with his fellow missionary Jean Séguin, a man from Auvergne five years older than he. Séguin was a gruff homebody, uncomfortable with the Indigenous languages and uncurious about their customs (attitudes that were typical of the Oblate missionaries). Patrick Kearney, an Irish Oblate brother, with the help of several employees, looked after the comfort, subsistence, and security of the two priests—as long as they were willing to stay within the limits of the fence that supposedly protected their meager gardens of uncertain yields. Surrounding them was the forest. The confined space of the small mission contrasted sharply with the vast open expanse of the lands of the Far North, most of it deserted and unexplored except by First Nations peoples.

The prospect of this blissful vagrancy made them depart with joy. I could hear their laughter under the vault of the forest, along with the songs whose sleeping echoes they roused. These cheerful notes clutched my heart, not out of envy or jealousy of the happiness they shared with the reindeer or migratory birds, but out of the failure of my own self-sacrifice, my voluntarily accepted hapless fate as a hermit and bachelor. I followed them from afar, which they realized, soothing my soul as a man without a wife, my heart as a father without children. After I paid this tribute to their rebellious nature and calm had been restored to my being through this deep relaxation, I returned home alone to resume my daily tasks.[19]

During his many years near the Arctic Circle, his priestly celibacy made him suffer, a stricture he came to see as appalling, describing it as "a wound of the Church," "a disciplinary measure adopted only in the ninth century, no doubt dictated by a century of disorder and abuse and which another century could completely abolish for the sake of public enlightment, a word from Rome being sufficient for that."[20] He found it almost impossible to resign himself to the sedentary lifestyle imposed on him by the Church; he would follow a group of Native trekkers as soon as he found an opportunity and under the slightest pretext, traveling with them through frozen lands, forest, and tundra, most often against the orders constantly reiterated by his superiors. Animated by perpetual dissatisfaction, no sooner had he arrived at his destination than he would contemplate leaving, envisioning himself as "a young missionary dreaming only of distant and dangerous excursions, geographical discoveries, and of converting the Indians."[21] But he could not resist the joys of the bed shared in the lodges in which the band took shelter every night during excursions that sometimes lasted weeks, nor could he control the attraction he felt for the Adonises among the Dené, especially the handsome Dzanyu, whom he baptized Hyacinthe, with all the solemnity of the Catholic ritual, naming him after the beautiful pagan youth whom Apollo and Zephyr fought over.

Two years after his arrival in the Far North, Émile Petitot confessed to his bishop that his heart was weak and his soul lacked strength, which prevented him from hardening himself against temptation. "What I dislike about myself, and this is the truth, is that I have a loving heart, too loving. No matter how much I feel repugnance in it against the fair sex, my obedience has failed in many encounters, I hereby confess my mea culpa."[22] Bishop Henri Faraud was an Oblate who hailed from Gigondas in France and whose aunt had been guillotined during the Revolution. His colleagues praised him more for his physical strength than for his intelligence. He considered Émile Petitot to be full of talent and zeal but also full of himself, doing as he pleased, submitting himself only reluctantly to the orders of his superiors, often disobeying, carried away by an ebullient nature. The young priest did not spontaneously confess the "shameful and very serious offense against morals" into which he had fallen; he was forced to do so by public rumors born of the incessant chattering of his "sweet thing," his "beloved," or simply his "boy," as Jean Séguin called the beautiful and wicked Hyacinthe, who saw no reason to keep a homosexual relationship secret.[23]

This "savage who professed to being so depraved" by making public the priest's sinfulness placed Émile Petitot in an untenable position.[24] His Catholic superiors shut their eyes to his conduct with alacrity, aware of the value of a missionary who "learned languages with truly surprising ease."[25] The Dené considered his inclinations to be merely an amusing oddity, not much stranger than the vows of life-long celibacy made by the priests, whom they viewed as a somewhat eccentric type of shaman. But Émile Petitot himself thought he was nothing but "a wicked priest, a disgraceful clergyman, a scandalous missionary."[26] Amazed by the simplicity and tolerance that the Dené people showed toward homosexuality, he no longer knew, as he once did, how to "sacrifice a special friendship for God" as soon as he sensed it blossoming.[27] He felt himself sinking deeper and deeper into the sin of his "criminal relations with the young man" and, from one relapse to another, found himself unable to resist the temptations that regularly appeared.[28] He then told all his fellow missionaries, even outside confession, about his "special friendships" with a frankness that his bishop once described as "frightening": he moaned, he wept, but his passion was stronger than his will.[29]

> This affliction will accompany me to the grave. In my heart is a wound that nothing can heal and that is ruining me. Sometimes I even feel my trust in God wavering in me. I reject this thought as impious, but there are some words in the Gospel that are so strong that they terrify me.[30]

In these moments of loving exaltation, Émile Petitot no longer really knew any limits; several times, on the pretext of giving witness to the "feelings of the savages" and "their progress in Christian knowledge," he translated letters he received from his young lover and sent them to be published in Catholic newspapers. "My Father, I do not see you but I take your hand, imagine this is happening. When you see this letter, you will imagine it. When you see what I write you here, pray a little for me right away, this very day. Then I will live, thank you, and if I see you again, I will be happy. It is because I love you that I speak this way. If you still remember Hyacinthe, write to me."[31] As for his ministry, it was shattered: his behavior contradicted head-on his appointed duty to preach to Indigenous peoples.

> I could not maintain a virtuous front at the same time that I felt pressured by the outcry of my conscience. I sensed too strongly that this hypocrisy was revolting to the savages. On a trip, I humbled myself before them; they laughed. It may have been reckless of me to confess

and condemn my conduct; they probably thought I was even viler after this act of penance; their sarcasm only increased. What should I do?[32]

He was filled with an intense sense of guilt but, despite repeated acts of contrition, he would temporarily forget his resolutions in the presence of Hyacinthe, who saw no harm in their relations ("In this tribe, with its gentle, kind character, cynicism"—which, in Émile Petitot's terminology, meant homosexuality—"was not a vice and no one was ashamed of his depravity, confident that it was shared by all").[33] As soon as Hyacinthe would leave, the missionary would be filled with remorse, thinking of the torments of hell and, above all, suspecting everyone—the Catholic priests, the Protestant staff at the fort, or local Native peoples—of ridiculing him, insulting him, slandering him.

He could not stop thinking that irony, sarcasm, and jealousy were hidden behind every word directed toward him.

> While externally the savages pray and show me signs of respect, apart from that, I am the object of a volley of insults and nasty jokes, which at first they did not hide from me, thinking I did not understand them.[34]

These torrents of ridicule were most likely imaginary, if we accept the opinion of his colleagues, who thought, on the one hand, that his secret was well kept (the Protestants at Fort Good Hope gave little credence to the circulating rumors, exclaiming, "Indians are such liars!"), and on the other, that the Native peoples calmly tolerated the missionary's misconduct and contradictions.[35] Confronted with the impossibility of resisting the call of the flesh, prey to mockery he sensed everywhere, Émile Petitot set out to find a way to redeem himself.

He first considered withdrawing to a Carthusian monastery, one of the most austere religious orders in which cloisture is permanent and silence almost absolute; along the same lines, he also sometimes considered joining the Trappists.[36] But perhaps this was merely a rhetorical strategy on his part to get his superiors to allow him to undertake what he considered to be the most assured way to rehabilitate himself in the eyes of God and men: to become a martyr to the infidel Inuit.[37]

★

In the second half of the nineteenth century, the Inuit remained beyond the reach of Christian missions. In open, continuous conflict with their Dené neighbors, they displayed marked mistrust of the latter's Catholic or Anglican allies. Émile Petitot set out on numerous expeditions to the Inuit, all of which ended in memorable failures, either because he was unable to reach their territory or because he was driven away as soon as he arrived. He wrote an entire book on the "Eskimos" in which he descanted magisterially on a wide range of subjects as if he had always lived among them, although in reality, he only had a series of isolated encounters, most often during journeys by river.[38] He substituted the insufficiency of his personal experience with reminiscences of books he had read but never credited.

For him, the Chiglit Inuit represented the height of savagery; he admitted to being fascinated by them since childhood.[39] He constantly asked his superiors to send him to them, initially to have the honor of being their first missionary (and their first ethnographer), and later to atone for his faults by becoming a martyr.

His writings reveal the intense emotion he felt when confronted with the Inuit, whom he described as "thieves and villains" and as living naked inside their homes, forming a polygamous people who "surpassed all others in license and immorality, imitating their ancestor through the cynicism of their vile practices."[40] From reading travelers' stories, the priest believed he could infer that "the crime of sodomy is permitted and practiced as a social institution."[41] The amalgam of unbridled sexuality and latent violence made for an explosive cocktail that distressed the missionary's overly sensitive nature. The very real threats he faced from certain individuals among the Inuit intensified his illusions of being persecuted to the utmost. As proof of this, he described a scene (whether true or false hardly matters) that supposedly took place when he camped in a snow igloo (which he never actually saw) and Iyoumatounak, a Chiglit Inuit shaman, proceeded to bewitch him.

> He crouched on the platform right in front of me and grabbed a flexible stick topped with a leather ball and having a strap attached, which he wrapped around the stick. He then began to sing, alternately unwinding and rewinding the strap on the spindle, which he twirled quickly. He began in a low, muffled tone and gradually became more animated, making the stick vibrate, shaking it angrily, rotating it sharply, and interspersing his song with harsh words and violent commands as if he were addressing a being subject to his orders. Soon Iyoumatounak, becoming more and more emboldened, shifted from songs to outcries, from outcries to shouts, and from shouts to howls. He kept changing "Yan! Yan! Eh!" in the same rhythm, accompanied by shaking, contortions, frightful grimaces, and some kind of convulsions. The unfortunate man was dripping sweat, wheezing, rolling his eyes, and foaming at the mouth; he tore off the few clothes he had on and, while drooling, got down on all fours like an animal. In sum, he was acting like a devil, and in truth, he was so beside himself that it was as if the man had disappeared to make way for a brute, but a thinking, talking brute. What could be more diabolical? While getting agitated in such an insane way, he shook and vibrated his magic spindle so much that he broke it. He replaced it with his long dagger and, all the while roaring and foaming like a possessed being, approached me little by little in

a state of overexcitation, impossible to describe. He was terrifying, horrible. His face had lost its human form, and his eyes seemed to want to stab me. He got so close to me that his face almost touched mine and I could feel his breath on my face. His gaze, like an angry hyena, bore into my eyes. . . . I glanced over at the Aoularenas [two women of the household]. Iyoumatounak's frenetic enthusiasm had infected them and won them over. They chanted and screeched the same "Eh! Yan! Yan! Eh!" in a tone so sharp and piercing that it made my ears ring. Like the circus performer, they seized their knives and rhythmically beat their upper thighs or the palm of their left hand with them. Their expressions were as vicious as his. It was as if all three of them were getting intoxicated with the noise, shouting, and contortions, just like others get intoxicated with alcohol or tobacco, to give themselves the courage to carry out some terrible deed. Undoubtedly some wicked scheme was being plotted against me.[42]

After this spectacular, hallucinatory passage, Émile Petitot, without any transition, calmly explained that it was enough for him to turn his back on this horde of "hyenas" to get them to immediately stop all displays of frenzy. It is hard to tell in these conditions whether the author was pushing the limits of his description or whether he simply wanted to portray the shaman in derisive terms. The point is that the intensity of the threat—and he actually was threatened by the Inuit on several occasions, most likely because of the presence of Dené with him—made a strong enough impression on him that he could fantasize about becoming a martyr to the Inuit, stabbed or lacerated by their long pagan daggers.

All my desire is to see my dear Eskimos again, a hope I dare hold onto. I do not fear death, although I have every reason to tremble in the face of my crimes, but if this death were a martyrdom, even if only a martyrdom of charity, I would welcome it with ecstasy. Oh, how I would like to die as a martyr! Do not admire these flights of ecstasy, there is perhaps more selfishness in them than love of God. It is simply that, through martyrdom, I would be baptized anew although, by contrast, my fear and remorse would remain with me. I dare hope, neverthless, that in this desire, there is at least a beginning of God's love.[43]

Émile Petitot never managed to stay with the Inuit long enough, so martyrdom was soon out of the question. However, the actual dangers he faced during these excursions gradually turned into imaginary threats, ones that were consistent with the incessant sarcasm and slander he thought he heard everywhere. His sporadic suspicions soon turned into a veritable persecutory delusion: everyone wanted to take his life and everywhere he saw a plot; sometimes it was the Inuit, sometimes the Dené, sometimes even the Protestants who wanted to kill him.

It is true that the Dené experienced one of the worst epidemics in their history during the winter of 1865–1866: scarlet fever killed nearly a quarter of the population.[44] However, it completely spared the missionaries, whom the Dené began to suspect from time to time of being able and willing to kill them by magical means. The doomsday atmosphere and sorcery accusations must have fueled Émile Petitot's nascent persecutory delusions, but it persisted long after the Dené, exhausted from the struggle, ceased their incriminations. According to the missionary, all the Inuit and Dené were thinking, "Let's kill them before they kill us." This projection, this "imaginary fear," became an obsession for him. "They want to kill me."[45]

★

In moral terms, Émile Petitot had become an exile. Catholic missionaries and, more generally, Christians, have long been regarded as strategic agents of Western imperialism, as people eradicating Native customs—their way of life, their unique form of social organization, their ceremonial traditions—and as beings blinded by an ethnocentrism that is both condescending and arrogant. All of this is certainly true. However, if we want to follow as closely as possible the train of Émile Petitot's delusional thinking, we must understand that the young reactionary priest was also at odds with his family and social environment. He viewed his departure to Canada as an affront that would lead his mother to the grave, "after six years of tears, anguish, and disappointment"—a mother who had never stopped repeating to him since he was little, "How ugly you are, my poor child, my, how ugly you are!"[46] Enthusiastic, voluble, and obstinate, he had embraced the vocation of a missionary less to convert and administer to pagans than to satisfy his desires for adventure and distant discoveries, desires that were only the reverse side of an essential dissatisfaction—social, spiritual, and sexual—that pushed him to leave behind, without regret, his future as a member of the petite bourgeoisie of Marseilles.

This exile, with his sad laughter, developed a sense of perpetual persecution ever since his first years in the Far North. To get a clear idea of the delusions from which Émile Petitot suffered—and which only intensified over the years—it is enough to read a letter he managed to get published in the September 1870 issue of the *Annales* of his congregation, taking advantage of the naïveté and ignorance of the leadership back in Marseilles. He detailed the anxieties that overtook him during a trip with the Dené from Fort Simpson to Fort Good Hope the previous year:

> I left Fort Providence on August 31, arrived at Fort Simpson on September 2, and immediately left to go to my beloved residence at Good Hope, from which I had been separated for over eight months. I breathed deeply upon returning; I had come close to never seeing

it again. Arriving close to some large rapids, the savages, twenty-one in number, who made up the crew of this boat, suddenly revealed a terrible plot. They wanted to throw me into the rapids. Almost all of them were nonbelievers and Hareskins. They complained that the priests were the cause of the illnesses and deaths that were decimating them, the beginning of which, they said, coincided with my arrival in their lands. Their intention, after getting rid of me, was to do the same to dear Father Séguin and Brother Kearney and then take to the forests. Already this spring, they had plotted the destruction of Good Hope and all the White people there; they had accused the Reverend Father Séguin of wanting to poison them. These are the consequences of the treacherous and insidious words of our separated brothers, the Protestants, employees of the Company.

I listened to the end without showing any fear or anger; then, when I had grasped all the threads of this plot and the murderers stood up to seize me, twenty-one against just me, sick and exhausted, I stood up and shouted to them that they could do with me what they wanted, I did not fear dying in such circumstances and would gladly give my life for them if they thought my death could give them health and long life. But, I said, I feared that this crime would only serve to ignite God's wrath against them; nevertheless, I would not cease to love them; my last cry would be "I love you," and I would further prove my love by praying for them when I was at the foot of my judge's throne. "And now," I said in conclusion, "have no fear, I will not defend myself. Do what you wish."

This outburst confused them so much that they wrung their hands in denial and declarations of respect, the excuse used by cowards. But they postponed the execution of their plan until nightfall, saying, "Now that he understood what we said, we have to carry it out for our own protection, otherwise he will sell us out to his compatriots, and the White people will kill us." Needless to say, I did not sleep that night. We were going adrift in cold and foggy weather; the four most frenzied among them were on the lookout to put their plan into action. Among the others, some displayed pity, but fear of their colleagues paralyzed their energy. Only one of them had enough courage to say, "Your plan makes my heart sick, my head is pounding; I will never take part in it." He wrapped himself in his blanket and lay down so he would not see me die. All night long, I prayed to God and the Blessed Virgin to not allow such a great crime to be committed. I recited my rosary the whole time. But I was prepared for death and oh! how joyous I was! ever so joyous to die a martyr. I was not worthy of it. After drinking hot tea, licorice, and sugar, etc., to make their hearts strong, as they said, my Hareskins, seeing that I stubbornly did not sleep, did not have the courage to carry out their plan. There were twenty-one of them against just one, certainly, but to have enough courage, they needed nighttime and for me to sleep. Until dawn, they were excitable; a word, a smile from me held them back immediately (since I carefully avoided giving them the impression that I was suspicious of them after they assured me they were not contemplating anything against me).

As day broke, they planned to throw me into some other rapids not far from Good Hope and, in anticipation, decided how they would divide up my belongings. When we got to the spot, they lost courage once again, so I arrived home safe and sound under the guidance of Our Lady of Good Hope, my protectress in this episode. Then they made plans to kill all three of us: Father Séguin, Brother Kearney, and myself. None of this was carried out; after plotting all that time over the past winter and summer, after having had the best opportunities to achieve their purpose, they dared not try anything.[47]

Jean Séguin collected the Dené's version after the barge arrived at the mission of Good Hope. They were unanimous in saying that Émile Petitot had once again gone mad: he had suddenly stood up and, in an intense state of exaltation, declared, "You can kill me with a gun or throw me into the water, I don't care, I am not afraid of death!" They then encircled him to prevent him from throwing himself into the water.[48]

If this time he suspected the Native peoples of plotting a scheme and planning to exterminate the Whites, sometimes it was the White people he imagined to be the source of a conspiracy and the driving force behind the Native peoples.[49] The only constant in his delirium was that his life was in danger, that others wanted to kill him, and that there was always "something behind the scenes."[50]

Upon reading this issue of the annals, the missionary's bishop was dismayed. Unlike the Oblate leaders, he knew well that the priest's fears were empty and the "ineffabilities," with their disjointed narrative, traitorous threats, insidious words, long-contemplated plots for the imminent destruction of the Whites, and the heroic posturing of a martyr, were "purely the effect of his troubled imagination and his obsessions that someone wants to kill him."[51] He immediately requested that the Church hierarchy refrain from publishing any more letters from Émile Petitot unless they were first examined by his immediate superiors.

These persecutory delusions, involving imaginary slander and death threats, took up more and more of the priest's daily life in the Arctic. His colleague Jean Séguin, obviously growing weary of the situation, regularly reported the details to his bishop.

> Father Petitot hears nothing but talk of death from all sides. I told you this spring that he thought he heard the savages around here say they wanted to kill him; when he went to Peel's River, he heard the same threats. When he arrived at the fort, it was the Gwich'in who were going to cut his throat; when he left, those in the mountains were the ones who were going to do this. He

arrived safe and sound at Lapierre House, where again there was nothing but death threats. When he boarded Youcon's barge, it was the same, but he reached the fort just fine; on his way back, wherever he encountered savages, there was only talk of death. In sum, everywhere he sees nothing but murderers. The savages, the hired help, the merchants, all want his life, he claims.[52]

However, the delusions seemed to evaporate during his stay in France from 1874 to 1876, so much so that the leaders of the Oblates of Mary Immaculate were of the opinion that internal conflicts must have been the source of exaggerated denunciations on the part of the missionaries of the Far North.[53] They therefore sent him back to Canada, where his delusions started up again. "The old stories and slander were too cold, so he invented new ones everywhere he went," and these constant recurrences partly justified the involuntary internment of Émile Petitot to a mental institution in 1882.[54] When the delusions seemed to fade once again after the priest was repatriated once and for all, the books he wrote in Mareuil-lès-Meaux did not detail any of his most phantasmagorical interpretations.[55]

★

On February 22, 1882, Dr. Perrault and Dr. Howard admitted Émile Petitot to the Longue Pointe Insane Asylum, located six miles from Montreal. The priest, then forty-seven years old, had come from faraway Saskatchewan. The director of the asylum, Thérèse de Jésus, quickly took him out of sight of the alienists (the common term at the time for those who were later called psychiatrists), leaving them only enough time to make a rather vague diagnosis of "mania."[56]

The first doctor to sign the admission order was François-Xavier Perrault, a French-speaking Canadian.[57] He was the resident doctor at Longue Pointe Asylum but was apparently unfamiliar with the latest works on mental illness. As a general practitioner, he had a bourgeois clientele in the Longue Pointe district, taking advantage of his position at the asylum, according to his detractors, simply to make ends meet. He seemed to consider Émile Petitot to be "of sane mind," suggesting to the priest that he was locked up only by order of the ecclesiastical hierarchy.[58] The second doctor who signed in Émile Petitot was Henry Howard, an English-speaking ophthalmologist and positivist in latent conflict with the Sisters of Charity.[59] He seemed to have only a loose conception of delusional states, considering them to be simply the consequence of organic lesions resulting from a long period of hereditary degeneration. Neither of them were current on recent studies, which would multiply over the coming decades, identifying the diagnostic framework in terms that were more or less equivalent: "Lasègue's disease," "moral madness," "reasoning madness," "systematized madness," or, according to Emil Kraepelin, "persecution paranoia," a label that gradually entered common parlance despite, or perhaps because of, its malleable contours. Émile Petitot's delusions and behavior manifested each of the most typical signs: intense narcissism, excessive pride, compulsive autodidactism, exaggerated jealousy, concealment reactions, frequent indecision, systematic overinterpretation, and, of course, imaginary persecution.

A few weeks before he was committed to the asylum, Émile Petitot went through a new series of delusional episodes and agreed to take another trip to France to rest and supervise the publication of various dictionaries of First Nations languages he had researched. During a long train ride with another missionary, Constantine Scollen, he wondered why they were headed for Montreal rather than going directly to New York. When he arrived at the door of the Oblates' house on February 21 at 8:30 pm, "in very good health and very calm," he was surprised to be "received with a sardonic and somewhat mysterious air, even a certain ironic coldness."[60] Nevertheless, he was given supper and shown a bed. The next day, he was put on a sleigh under some pretext and, without giving him time to react, the director of the asylum, notified by the Oblates, had him locked up against his will. As Émile Petitot later told his sister, this was done

> without the doctor here finding me ill, without anything in my conduct, in the space of so few hours, providing any plausible reason. But there are some who know very well how to use injustices to skew a procedure and arm themselves beforehand with all the desirable opportunities and recommendations, so they seem to follow the procedure with as much legitimacy as possible. This is an odious betrayal and an unspeakable breach of trust.[61]

The Longue Pointe Insane Asylum, a four-storey brick building topped by three domes, consisted of a central building flanked by two wings that were gradually being extended, with their ends still under construction. Dr. Perrault's office, where Émile Petitot was briefly received, was located in the central building near a reception hall, a large kitchen, and a pharmacy where the Sisters of Charity took care of two hanging skeletons, from which they learned the anatomy of the human body. The symmetrical wings, one for women and the other for men, contained identical corridors, bedrooms, and dining rooms on three floors. Everything was clean, well furnished, and relatively quiet, even in the dormitories interspersed between the rows of single rooms. It is likely that Émile Petitot never ventured into the semibasement or, worse, the fourth floor at the top, where the Sisters locked up the most refractory "lunatics," those with severe, chronic mania. The gloomy corridor was still crowded with the mentally ill leaning by the dozens against the walls, some sitting on restraint chairs nailed to the ground, others wearing a straitjacket, and most of the others restrained by iron or leather handcuffs attached to a belt. "If they are untied, they take off their clothes," the Sisters explained, offended at the indecency.[62] The windowless cells were bare, dirty, and nauseating; the residents were confined within them, suffocating and handcuffed at the wrists and ankles. "A cabinet of horrors," a visiting English doctor said the following year, outraged.[63]

Although Émile Petitot was held against his will, he did not share the fate of those who were "raving, dangerous, and otherwise refractory."[64] He could hear them scream day and night but did not mingle with them. He admitted that the Grey Nuns surrounded him with kindness; he was, in fact, one of the paying residents.

> Nevertheless, oh, unbearable shame! I find myself in the midst of the mad! I am locked up every night; it is true that I undergo gentle treatment, but I know it is not necessary; I will have to suffer the stigma of insanity no matter what kind of life I adopt afterward.[65]

While most of the letters he wrote from the asylum testified only to very real persecutions, he sometimes wondered, in all seriousness, whether Constantine Scollen, the Oblate missionary who had led him to Montreal and whom he described as "a miserable captain of industry," had taken on his name and was trying to impersonate him, "something incredible and iniquitous to the highest degree."[66] He was not released from internment until thirteen months later.

Figure 3. Émile Petitot wearing Dinjié clothing in the photography studio of L. E. Desmarais in Montreal, Canada, undated (1874?). Photograph courtesy of Archives Deschâlets, Richelieu, Canada.

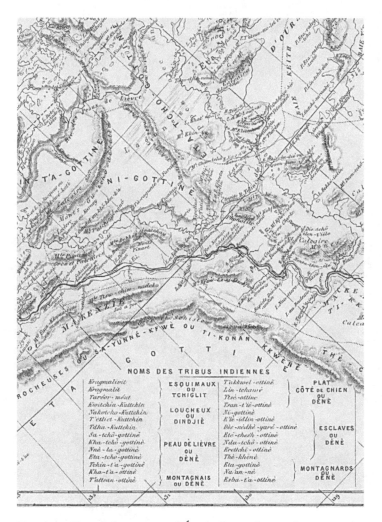

Figure 4. Detail from map of Émile Petitot's expeditions to the Dinjié and northern Dené, 1862–1873 (based on drawing by Jules André Arthur Hansen, *Bulletin de la société de géographie* 10 [1875]). © Zones sensibles, used with permission.

CHAPTER TWO

Interpretation Delusions
Israelites of the North Pole

On the deck of the ship that led him for the first time to America, in April 1862, Émile Petitot, in his capacity as a Catholic priest, was asked to consult on a bizarre dispute, despite his young age and the inadequacy of his ecclesiastical studies, during which he made a brief alliance with a Jewish passenger to contradict a Protestant one. He had just left the Major Seminary of Marseilles, a reactionary institution if ever there was one, closed to profane matters and where only a literal interpretation of the Bible was taught.

> In the third-class steerage were more than three hundred Irish and German passengers, who were emigrating to Canada. Among them was a Jew who was dressed in a Polonaise frock coat lined with fox fur and wearing a kind of kolbach hat. He said he was Asian, although he answered to the name of Müller. He was a stone merchant who affected the deepest religious indifference, except when Israel's honor was at stake. In his case, I must say, in all fairness, that he didn't know a thing about human respect. And he was always sure he was right. Mr. Müller made more noise on his own than his two hundred and ninety-nine steerage companions. He came and went, orating in German, English, Italian, and Syriac. He settled all questions in an authoritarian tone, seemed to

hate the English, extolled the Americans, and repeated himself incessantly like parrot's chatter. His aplomb, his quips, his feigned anger, and especially his jeweler's box enabled him to be admitted to the quarterdeck, where third-class passengers had no access.[1]

After tea on the morning of April 10, when the ocean was somewhat agitated, Émile Petitot saw the "worthy son of Israel" advancing toward him with a hesitant stride, his hand holding the railing a little more tensely with each step. The man immediately addressed him in a rattled voice, omitting greetings and formalities:

"My dear priest," cried the Israelite, "I want you to be the judge of a dispute. I'm sure that your opinion will fit with mine."

"What is it about, sir?"

"A judgment rendered by an English jury in Canada against one of my coreligionists named Jacob ***. Over there is Mr. Cotnam, a respectable English Canadian from Quebec, who has been telling me for a full quarter of an hour that the Patriarch Jacob used deceit and lies to obtain Isaac's blessings. He supports the absurd view of the court's recent ruling in favor of an Israeli named Solomon against Jacob, whom the first accused of fraud in a commercial transaction. Jacob desperately denied that he had acted fraudulently. Solomon swore that there had been deceit and duplicity. He argued to the jury that, since the Patriarch Jacob was the first liar, it was a long tradition in the synagogue that all Jews who bear the same name have inherited this paternal quality. A simple phenomenon of atavism, Sir.

"Mr. Cotnam said, 'Presented with this testimony, the Canadian jury would not have hesitated to convict Jacob***.' Can you believe that? And that's what he calls proof!" cried Mr. Müller, flushed with anger. "You see, it outrages me, it exasperates me, and I ask for your testimony! What do you think of this reasoning, Sir?"[2]

The third-class Jewish passenger (who may have been a Hasidic, if the hat that Émile Petitot called a "kolbach" by analogy was actually a kolpik, a kind of traditional fur cap) was thus seeking, perhaps naïvely, the support of a Catholic to counter the anti-Semitism he encountered at breakfast from a myopic Anglican used to traveling quietly in the comfort of first class. Müller's reaction was driven by an indignation undoubtedly accentuated by the lurching of the ship. The priest, after listening to the account of the quarrel with a smile on his face, now laughed.

> "If anything," I said to him, "the little story that Mr. Cotnam told you comes from an English paper, probably from the columns of *Punch* or *Comic Clippings*, and I think he took a spoof for a serious news item.
>
> "As for the reasoning you are telling me, it is neither Israelite, nor Catholic, nor even Protestant; for the Protestants believe as well as we do in the holiness of the Patriarch Jacob. If this implausible judgment were rendered, it would not have convicted Jacob of a lie. . . ."
>
> "I knew it!" exclaimed the exultant Asian Jew, "I knew perfectly well that you, a priest, would share my opinion, as would all the priests in the universe!"[3]

The ridiculous argument bore no intrinsic interest whatsoever. It nevertheless foreshadowed the social and religious coordinates in which Émile Petitot found himself thrown during his mission below the Arctic Circle. For the enemy of the Catholic missionary in these distant lands was the figure of an Anglican minister, whom he considered guilty of stealing unfaithful Native souls from the Catholics through patently underhanded, ignoble means. And, more specifically, the natural allies to which Catholics ought to attach themselves, as part of their mission, were none other than the Hebrew people. Émile Petitot, in fact, thought that the Dené were Jewish.

★

Only a few months after his arrival at the missions of Canada's Far North, he was surprised at the radical difference between the Dené (whom the missionaries of the time often called Montagnais) and the image he had formed, through his reading as a teenager, of American Plains Indians proudly wearing a crown of feathers and riding a galloping horse bareback. The young priest began to question the vague ideas that had unexpectedly slipped into his luggage:

> The divergence of traditions that exists between the Montagnais and the other redskins further south, a total divergence in language and habits, leads me to believe that the Montagnais are a distinct race and that not all nations in North America are Indigenous. I would be happy to have some basics of the Hebrew or Syriac language with me. With what little I know of the Montagnais language and what the good Lord will let me learn of it, if he lets me live, who knows if it might be possible to make curious discoveries about the origin of these peoples?[4]

The speculation had not come out of nowhere. Vital Grandin, the Oblate bishop and missionary who accompanied Émile Petitot from Marseilles to Canada (and who ended up, twenty years later, having him interned in a mental institution in Montreal), already thought, based on some Dené customs and certain lexicalized expressions in their language, that "if the Montagnais are not descended from the Hebrews, they are at least descended from some people who interacted with them."[5] As for Émile Grouard, Émile Petitot's other travel companion, he asserted that "all missionaries, Catholics and Protestants, who had regular contact with the peoples of North America, noticed the similarities between Indians and Hebrews."[6] The idea was thus already in the air among the Oblates and others. This should come as no surprise, however, if we consider that the missionaries of the time taught Indigenous peoples the chronology of the Catholic Scale, a Biblical story in images that traced the creation of the world back to a little less than six thousand years ago.[7] Within such a narrow framework, in which the Adamic origin of humanity was taken as self-evident, cultural analogies could hardly be interpreted as anything other than the result of a combination of migration and diffusion processes; the idea of evolutionary convergence was not even up for consideration.

★

Nan digal'é. Inkfwin-wélay ya–kkètchiné klané narwet. Inl'ègé ténéyu enli, inl'égé yénnéné enli. Khiyué nigunti. Ttasin yakhési, ttasin kkè tchonkhéninya, ékhu yéra kkinayendifwéwer xhè ékhu yayési. Inkfwin-wétay bétchilékwié nné yaési, ékhu ttasin xénna-xhô-wé héni, béhonnè tcholléyé, éyi la nnè kkê nilpénitchu; kwila ninitchu, ekhu kohannè konéguntié anagotti. Ekhulla naokhé, tragè, dingi, ehttsen-tragé ékra adjia xhé, ayhè natigal'é. Eyitta nné nézin runhéyékkwé.[8]

The creation. Seated-at-the-Zenith dwells at the base of Foot-of-Heaven. One of them is a man, the other a woman. Their clothes are very beautiful, made of choice furs. They create all things through their dreams and the power of their medicine. They lie down, they sleep, and everything gets done. At the very beginning, Seated-at-the-Zenith sent his young people to make the earth. Over the chaos, they spread something supple, soft, and silky, similar to a tanned elkskin. In this way, they beautified the earth a bit. After removing this covering, they spread it out a second time, and when the earth came out from underneath, it was even more beautiful. Then he sent his servants to do the same thing three times, four times, five times, six times, and then the earth was completed.

Story by Lizette Khatchôti, Dené Hareskin,
January 1870[9]

★

Unlike his Oblate colleagues, who only noticed the similarities between Hebrew and First Nations societies in passing, Émile Petitot devoted abundant energy to the theoretical and historical problem of the origin of Indigenous peoples in Canada, especially the Dené among whom he lived. His passionate temperament, combined with his keen curiosity and fragmentary knowledge, fueled an interest that soon became an obsession. Apparently blind to the signs of anti-Semitism that was festering at the time, he made use of every possible argument to prove that the Dené should be considered the descendants of the Hebrews of the Old Testament.[10] At first, after overcoming his initial repugnance, he became convinced that the physiognomy of the Dené was similar to that of Jewish people.

The Montagnais can be depicted as follows: an elongated, pointed, and elevated head; long, straight, stiff, and shiny black hair, parted in two on the forehead and falling in long strands onto the shoulders. Women do not even bother to part their hair, letting it hide their faces. The Montagnais forehead is receding, conical. and indented on the temples, although it is quite high; their eyes, brown and burning, are slightly slanted and astonishingly fixed; their eyelids are large and heavy, their cheekbones protruding, and their chin singularly pointed. They have a wide mouth, always open and with fleshy lips, swollen in some, prominent in others; small, well-made feet and hands; and legs that are lean and curving outward. In short, I find nothing of the features of the Malay and Chinese I have had occasion to see;

rather, their high cheekbones, their pointed heads, and their straight hair make them fit into the Semitic race. The illustrious A. de Humboldt has already noted, with Nott and Morton, through examining their skulls, that they do not belong to the Mongolian family. As for me, I cannot help but see a Jewish physiognomy in their profile.[11]

Perhaps it should be recalled that Émile Petitot, in citing the work of Samuel G. Morton and Josiah C. Nott, oddly invoked the American founders of "scientific racism," who considered human races as separate species with their own physical and intellectual characteristics that could not be modified, each race having been the product of a distinct act of creation by God. This was a typically American theory of polygenism; in most of the scientific traditions in other countries, polygenic racism led instead to a form of positivist atheism. Since many Americans needed to reconcile God, science, and slavery, their racism may have held a certain allure at the dawn of the nineteenth century. Of course, Émile Petitot professed the Catholic doctrine, that is, Adamic monogenism: according to the Bible, humans had only been created once. Nonetheless, his undernourished autodidactism easily ignored the epistemological assumptions underlying the works he was reading, using them only to support his own position that the Dené, as evident even in their physiognomy, were descendants of the ancient Hebrews, more precisely, the "tribes of Israel lost after their captivity in Babylon."[12]

In fact, Émile Petitot went even further: among the ten lost tribes of Israel listed in the second book of Kings, he came to identify the one from which he believed the Dené descended. The reasoning that undergirded all his propositions could be reduced to a simple lexical approximation:

Using what I already know about their eminently Hebrew practices and customs, I do not hesitate to

consider the American Dané or Dené to be the sons
of Dan-ben-Yacoub, the Danites. I hear a universal
concert of protest mounted against me over this. The
superstitious, the faint-hearted, the enemies of the
Bible and of the Hebrew tradition will not fail to raise
an outcry.[13]

The Dené were thus descended from the tribe of Dan, the
fifth son of Jacob, a tribe that long ago, after the destruction
of the Kingdom of Israel, crossed the Bering Strait to settle
in the forests and tundra of Canada's Far North. When
the priest revealed this secret identity of the Dené—whom
he henceforth called, imperturbably, Arctic Danites—he
was already aware of the polemical nature of his position,
having revealed it to members of his congregation as well
as to the Parisian scientific community. During his visit to
France between 1874 and 1876, he had the opportunity to
make public his argument about the Hebrew practices and
customs of the Dené, particularly at the first International
Congress of Americanists, held in Nancy in 1875. There,
before an audience that was partly positivist, partly
Catholic, he displayed his direct, intimate familiarity with
the Indigenous peoples of boreal America. This contrasted
eloquently with the erudite compilations that his scientific
opponents were content to make, resulting exclusively
from their frequenting libraries and perusing books, which
prompted him to call them "reading-room scholars" and
"fireside savants."[14] Although he was not invited by the
conference organizers, he was thrust forward by the Catholic
wing at the last minute to speak. At this inaugural assembly,
half scientific, half diplomatic, Émile Petitot presented a list
of twenty-nine customs that he saw as identical between the
ancient Hebrews and the Arctic Danites, summarizing his
twelve years of research and reflection.[15]

From this heteroclite list, in which each Dené tradition
was matched with a Latin quotation from the Old Testament,
a small selection should be illustrative, laid out in an order

almost as arbitrary as the one adopted by the missionary: the taboo on dog meat; the separation of spouses for forty days after childbirth; marriage with a sister-in-law; the weaning of children after three years; the ritual repugnance toward human remains; the sequestration of women when they were subject to "their natural infirmity"; the twelve-moon calendar; solitary childbirth; the bleeding of game (their meat was therefore kosher); the knowledge of snakes, although, in the Dené case, "there are none in their country, which is buried under the snow and ice for nine months of the year"; the belief in the immortality of the soul; the recognition of a divine triad in the animalized form of three mythical eagles; the idea that "the woman is the author of the evils of humanity"; the nocturnal festival of the renewal of the moon, exactly like the Jewish Passover; and so on.[16]

★

Innié-ton dènè étiéyonlini, ékhu étié dènè yakhinlé, kruluyakunyon illé enkharé, fwin étié akhinla. Eyiyitta èta-khédété: étié dènè yawélé, ékhu dènè étié akhétchya, déti. Eyitta trinttchanadey yonlini, khu-tatsénétrè dènè kkéèn: krulu éyini bétatsénétrè bé kfwen tséhali illé. Eyunné la tl'in yawélé, ékhu dènè-khinlé; éyitta tl'in ttsintséwi, ékhu tl'in dènè ra-lakhéyéta. Bénigunlay wéré tl'in du bératsédéti, dènè xhè nadé oyi, khuxè natsézé. Eyitta tl'in tséwéxié illé. Kotsintè yénikfwen, ékhu dènè kkéèn béra tsénétré.[17]

The taboo of unclean animals. In the beginning of time, the people of today were reindeer and the reindeer we eat were humans, but humans who had no spirit and could not kill a single animal. That is why they switched roles: humans became reindeer and reindeer were transformed into humans. This explains why we do not sleep with pure animals (and why we eat them) as if they were human creatures. But we must not eat the flesh of those with whom we sleep: those enemies whom we call ghosts, madmen, and courtesans were originally dogs that were later transformed into humans. That is why we make dogs suffer and we make them the slaves of humans, but we do not kill them; it is a crime to kill a dog, because they are our former enemies and therefore human beings. And so we sleep with dogs as well as with humans.

Story by Lizette Khatchôti, Dené Hareskin,
January 1870[18]

★

The last items in Émile Petitot's list of analogies between the Dené and ancient Hebrews ventured into the field of religious ceremonies and conceptions, which were, in the final analysis, his specialty. He had much more to say on the subject:

The religion of the Montagnais, if one can give this name to their scenes of dissimulation, consists of a crude fetishism that I will call Jewish fetishism, since it is mixed with traditions and prescriptions that obviously have a Jewish origin. . . . A fast in preparation for receiving the spirit; sin as the cause of sickness and death that would follow; the compulsory confession of the sick to recover health; the power to bring the spirit down to the earth and to eradicate sin. Are these not the vestiges of Judaism?[19]

If the shamanism of the Dené was ultimately no different from "Jewish fetishism," their numerous mythological accounts, which Émile Petitot was the first to collect, were allegedly saturated with survivals from the Bible. As the editor of a short review of Petitot's work in this field commented sardonically, "The author, self-taught, is among those who, when it comes to Biblical criticism, are bold and candid."[20]

In their traditions, there is an excellent version of the universal flood, connected to Zoroastrian ideas; the spread of languages in Babel; the knowledge of the longevity of the first people; the presence of giants in their land of origin; the fall of the solitary first human couple through the fault of the youngest; the redemption of humanity by the son of the divinity, however much it was an animal: an enormous eagle as white as snow, called Otôàlé, Immensity and Innocence. Their ideas are thus fundamentally Aramaic and Biblical. So far, however, these are no different than what is found universally. But some Dené heroes are reminiscent of Moses, Abraham, and Samson; others recall Jonas, David, and Tobie.[21]

In a letter to Laurent-Achille Rey, his former professor at the Major Seminary of Marseilles,[22] Émile Petitot courageously sketched a first synthesis of his mythological studies, which clearly revealed his enthusiasm over having made a revolutionary discovery.

Our Indians are the remains of the tribes of Israel taken into captivity. Without preconceived ideas or any systematic bias, it is fortunate that time, chance, and the taste for ethnological studies have led me to make what I consider to be a discovery. I have materials in front of me to write a lengthy book about it and believe I have enough evidence to make me certain of the fact. I have gathered most of the traditions of the Montagnais, Dogribs, Hareskins, and Kutchin. They are the same in substance and complement each other like the four Gospels to form a whole that is the Biblical account as it stands. There are three classes among these traditions:

1. Pure and simple stories devoid of any fiction, such as the episode of manna, the passage of the Red Sea, the death of the first-born Egyptians, the Passover ceremony, the law given on Sinai, the entire story of

Samson, the sacrifice of Aaron, the flood, the star of Bethlehem, etc., etc.

2. Denatured narratives in which animals replace humans, but the main character, the Biblical one, shows through clearly and with the same attributes as he has in our holy books: these are the stories of Abraham, Lot and the Sodomites, Moses throughout, David, Gideon, Judith, Tobias, etc., etc.

3. Parables or fables in which it is very easy to recognize a moral purpose and a hidden meaning, unknown now to the Indians, but about which their ancestors must not have been ignorant: these are the stories of redemption, the fall of man, the deliverance of the Jewish people, etc., etc.[23]

The "etceteras" were now tumbling out in pairs. His correspondent (who would soon become the first chaplain of Montmartre, making his flock atone for the unholy horrors of the Paris Commune, the news of which provoked anxiety and indignation among the Oblates everywhere) could easily imagine the potentially exceptional size of the "big book" in preparation. At the end of his letter, Émile Petitot referred to Dené linguistics: beyond the lexical roots that he considered identical between the Dené and Hebrew languages, based on countless lists he drew up (because "the primitive and universal language, by decomposing in the plains of Sennar, divided without being lost"), he discovered a common origin even in the morphologies of their languages: "The various dialects that make up the Dené-Dindjié language are only distinguished by the change of vowels, the consonants being prefixed as in Hebrew."[24]

Physionomy, language, technology, customs, religion, mythology—the doubt was no longer an option for the frenetic spirit of the polymath priest: the Dené could only be "Arctic Jews." In fact, this was the title he originally wanted to give his magnum opus on the subject, finally entitled *Accord des mythologies dans la cosmogonie des Danites arctiques* (Concordance of Mythologies in the Cosmogony of the Arctic Danites).[25] Published in 1890, this work drowned in lush erudition and unbridled analogies that led to fanciful conclusions, almost impossible to summarize, by implementing the method he always cherished, the common thread of all his studies: "To seek the same belief in the four parts of the world."[26]

★

Nan dugunli. Tchapéwi wékhiéné na-dènè honné-déwa kwotlan ensin tri-tchô l'atradéha rottsen nadéta-yinlé, ittchié itta, inkfwin ttsen. Ekhuyé fwané narwô ittchié itta, wékhiéné yékkiéttcha atti itta. Etaxon ensin tri-tchô édélyel koïtli akhi tri nan elpen adjya; tchon tchô dellé. Etèwékwi wétchanré, akhi kohanzé tri elpen itta tédi nan taré elpen akutchia. Ekhilla Tchapéwi, l'atradéha gunli dessi, éyédi l'akké-inhé narwô ensin, minla xhè trinttchanadey tcho dunè tcho tta triyéyinhè éyini la kron-yéllé, axhé nankkié na nikhié nilla. Kruli kohannéttsen tru naépel itta, ettsendôw xiéni tchô wétsi wékkié t'intt- charadey onkhiékhédetté ninilla la, xiéni xhè taéllé adjia. Fwa gott- sen tchan delléni akhi tru tta tchi kondowé-ttsen nétchay otarèttsen elpen. Eyitta awondé unli illé nila, nan inkra tséniwen; khulu nan unli illé la anagotti.[27]

The flood. An old man withdrew to a strait connecting two immense seas in the north. There he lived alone, angry and sullen. Suddenly, he heard rumbling from the gulf as if it were going to rise up and spill out over the earth. Torrential rains fell from the sky while the old man slept, making the water in the seas rise higher and higher, soon covering this small piece of land. Then the old man stood up and straddled the strait with one leg on each side. With his broad hands, he fished out the animals and people being swept into the waters and moved them to dry land. But the waters kept on rising, so he made a huge raft on which he placed each species of animal, male and female. After the waters had covered the whole earth, the raft floated away. The rains fell for such a long time that the waters rose above the highest peaks of the rocky mountains. The situation became unbearable and all the animals on the raft yearned for dry land. But no more dry land was left.

Story by an anonymous storyteller,
a Dené Dogrib of Great Bear Lake, 1868[28]

★

By 1868, Émile Petitot's persecution complex was firmly entrenched. He constantly imagined slander and death threats from all sides, regularly putting his life in danger. His unpredictable behavior and unfounded accusations drove his colleagues at the mission of Our Lady of Good Hope, Jean Séguin and Patrick Kearney, to the point of utmost exasperation.

He was convinced that people were laughing at him and wanted to kill him. In those years, he also began to suffer from "nervous attacks," episodes of "mania" when he lost control of himself and locked himself in his room, forbidding anyone to enter. He would leave only after reaching a state of intense fury, when he would rail against his colleagues and attack them, then flee alone on foot through the snow, to the point that it was sometimes necessary to punish him, locking him up and monitoring him.[29] In 1870, Jean Séguin reported that Émile Petitot had suffered four episodes of mania, each one "more and more intense," most of them during the winter months, when darkness was continuous and temperatures hovered around thirty or even forty degrees below zero. Séguin feared that the missionary would "lose his mind altogether."[30]

During these bouts, Émile Petitot became a graphomaniac, even more than usual, filling up hundreds of pages in an exalted state of mind. According to Jean Séguin,

Father Petitot had another bout of madness. From Christmas until January 27, he worked night and day, I suppose to make all the stories of the savages coincide with the Bible. From the few examples he told us from time to time, we could judge that it was quite a lot of nonsense. But it was clear to him and that was all that mattered. He has scribbled on both sides of all the paper we had left.[31]

In this state, he amassed his intuitions and discoveries about Dené Judaism to such an extent that he sometimes wondered a posteriori if his writings were driven by the leaps of his "maniacal imagination," for example, in the field of linguistics, only to dismiss the hypothesis immediately:

I have resumed my studies on the Dené languages. I believe I have made a singular and important discovery in the comparative and analytical study of these dialects, which has unfolded a vast, marvelous world before my eyes. I get involved in logic, metaphysics, and philosophy when I engage in this seemingly dry study. I do not think this is a game of my imagination, since, far from racking my brain to find the order I am talking about, it reveals itself to me through the analogy of the words and even the letters. I pushed this exercise to its limits to make sure that I was not being fooled by a maniacal imagination, and my opinion was confirmed more and more. The complete analysis of the whole language, which I am currently doing, by giving me all the root words and letters, confirms this theory.[32]

Émile Petitot spent his nights writing. "What is he writing? I don't know," Jean Séguin reported. "All his papers are always under lock and key. So that no one will surprise him, he shuts himself up in his room with a latch."[33] Émile Petitot mistrusted Jean Séguin, to whom he attributed all evils, either because he thought his colleague was defaming him in the eyes of the ecclesiastical hierarchy (which was true), or because he suspected Jean Séguin was plotting, along with Indigenous and Métis individuals, to kill him. Not surprisingly, this led Émile Petitot to isolate himself within the walls of his room and to hide all of his activities, including the most trivial. "I suspect," Jean Séguin continued, "that he is working on some text, probably on what he calls *The Jews of the North Pole*. When we need to enter his room, he makes sure to close up everything before the door is opened, leaving only one book open in front of him, but we can easily hear the rustling of the paper."[34]

★

In'la tchinkié niguntiyama-trié kkié kkinata-yinlé; akhi l'ué-tchô trikkié tanémi. "L'uè-tchô s'édintl'a!" yendi tchinkié. Xunésin tra édédétri itta l'uétchiyénétla nila. Trarè dziné wétchôn yé yékendi. Eyi akron tchinkié wétiézé inl'asin etsé nila, trinba kkinatsiédédélla; édaxon l'uétchô naxoretti, akhi wétchon rottsen wétchilé dahiyé adi koïtli: "Enba! enba! étin! Kondowéttsèn étriénétti, l'ué-tchô Koji! Wé tchon sé kkié dinkkron," enni. "Ejitta néranitadénihon, enba, l'ué-tchô ttsen né khié-kkiéwé wéttsen naninkka éyixhè djian-kottcha ttsen krasédintpi," éné, adu tsié xhè. Eyitta éttiédékhu wékkié kkiéwé kkéétton ensin l'ué tchô ttsen nayénékka ayhé khiétchinklu uyitron, déti nila. Ekhu tchinkié khié iltchu itta, éyer ottala l'ué tchô nayé nékhu nadli, hétsédi. T'ama nayénékhu, kkatchiné él'aniwô, krulu réna tté la. Eyitta l'ué tchô untlazé binniyé-illé itta, wétché xhè tru nanéyinkka. Eyer ottala tradétcho nétchay anaudjya. Tchi la héni ettsentaré dédétrin, ékhu tékokkié nadékli itta, nan otaélpen nadli. Tchinlkié wé tiézé kkratcho éyi khié la du triyaïnron, déti.[35]

Jonas Dené. A young man was walking along the edge of the sea when a large fish appeared on the surface of the water. "Big fish, swallow me up!" shouted the young man. He immediately threw himself into the waves and was swallowed up by the sea monster, who kept him inside his body for three days. Meanwhile, the young man's sister went to the shore and wailed constant lamentations, mourning the cruel fate of her younger brother. Then suddenly, the big fish appeared and came to the surface of the sea. From the depths of the monster's entrails, a voice was heard shouting, "Oh, Sister, Sister, how miserable I am in the belly of the big fish! His bowels are burning me, ah! I beg of you, throw one of your shoes at the big fish, holding the laces in your hands, and pull me out of here." So the girl untied one of her shoes and threw it at the monster, holding the long laces in her hands. The big fish opened its huge mouth and swallowed the shoe. The young man immediately grabbed it and his sister pulled him toward her by the laces, causing the monster to vomit up her brother. It vomited him onto the shore, more dead than alive, but safe and sound nonetheless. Then the monster, irate to see its prey escape, struck the sea with its tail so vigorously that huge waves welled up. They rose like mountains and fell back to the earth, swallowing it up and flooding everything. Only the two young people were saved.

Story told by Sakranetrawotra, Dené Dogrib, June 1864[36]

★

Bishop Isidore Clut, on his way to the Good Hope mission to verify, among other things, Jean Séguin's allegations, confirmed the latter's suspicions about Émile Petitot.

After his great crisis last winter, he wrote strange things for a whole month without stopping. His writing involves a lengthy commentary on the savages' stories by way of the Bible and the Jewish people from whom the Dené are descended.

He keeps everything under lock and key, but I was able to glimpse some passages of his writing and some passages from his diary. He is now at Chapter 43. I fear that some day, he will have some things published that will be regrettable for our missions.[37]

A few months later, after discovering that letters from Émile Petitot with a rather paranoid tone appeared in an issue of the annals of the Congregation of the Oblates of Mary Immaculate, the bishop explained to the superior general why nothing more of his should be published:

This priest wrote many inaccuracies, false interpretations, etc., which have unfortunately been reproduced. He has a huge journal and a book on Indian traditions divided into three volumes. I could only read a few passages, without his knowledge, but I know enough to beg of you to never let him publish these works. Among other things, there are some unspeakable things he wrote in the interval between his two great bouts of madness in 1871. It would take too long to explain it. He keeps everything locked up. Father Séguin remarked that dear Father Petitot's spirit had been disturbed since 1868.[38]

For Isidore Clut, it had become obvious that "the study that the Reverend Father Petitot made on the origin of the Indians, their traditions, and the roots of their language was the cause of his madness," and he feared more than anything else that the missionary would have his research published.[39]

It would be a great misfortune for our congregation and our missions if such works were to appear, for judging by passages I read without the knowledge of Father Petitot, who does not intend to show his works to anyone, he narrates his delusions and his dreams in them. He has written down everything that came to his imagination during the days of his crisis. It reads like a story of *A Thousand and One Nights*. It's enough to make one pity him.[40]

★

Tchapévi nné navési kotlan sin, dunié l'atcho nné tadinni ttsen nago-dévi-yinlé. Ekhu éyet ttasin inkhulé, inwulédé nétcha-tchôyavési yinlé. "Alla dintoré tru naxiékké-inron nidé, tédi niyé kké dévité-woléni aëkranon," akhétiyinlé. Eyédi kottsen niva-illé denkroni gunl'i, déti. Akhu niyé kontonné ya ttsen niva-illé tavéhon, ensin, xunédi chiéyigé dunié kkètséklu koïtli, ékra atséti koïtli: "Ekhulla naxiéxétié l'ékkèttcha akhinténaxié, kotéyé éten aguntté," akhu-tséti. Dunié ttsékhédatl'a, dadégé khu adjya. Enttey la, dékroni gunl'i, déssi, dunié vinan dadékfwé, éyini khé yadikkron xhè kratatl'a adja, pfé yadétral, chi éhkkènél'é xu kkron tchô gottsen kradatl'a; ékhu gottsen gul'a-akutchia éyi kokl'aë ontrié tcho intrenyédé niwéha.

Ekhu duniékhé yakodédjié ensin él'attsen-khédétié, axodéyoné ti gokké tiéatié. Eyédi kottsen, déti, dunié l'ékhéuvéppuon illé.[41]

The collapse of the mountain; or, the multiplication of languages. All the people took refuge on high ground, a tall mountain, where they built something round in the shape of a tube, like your stovepipe, but immense and towering. "If the flood comes again and covers the earth, we will take refuge in this high fort," they said. Coal mines were burning near this huge stone tube. After they had built their fort on high ground, they suddenly heard terrible voices from the side of the mountain mocking them and sneering, "Your language is no longer the same; your language has completely changed!" they said with a sinister laugh. The people flinched in shock and began trembling with fear.

At the same time, the coal mines bellowing with smoke around them caught fire, rocks exploded, and the mountain split open, spewing forth a huge fire. It then collapsed with a deafening crash, and in its place nothing was left but vast bleak plains blanketed with smoking debris. The people, stupefied and filled with dread, dispersed in small groups in all directions, no longer able to understand each other.

Story told by Tétiwotra, Montagnard Dené chief, known as The Full-Throated One, 1869[42]

★

At the Longue Pointe Insane Asylum, Émile Petitot understood that his studies and their supposedly scandalous nature were the main reason for his internment. "The Bishop admitted to me that what people feared most about me were my writings. Do they fear the light?"[43] Later, having been relieved of his vows, he managed to publish part of his memoirs, but the last two volumes, which had been ready for print ever since 1894, were never published; they ended up being burned along with most of his papers upon his death.[44] The ex-missionary felt the need to defend himself from accusations by members of his former congregation, as well as from his Parisian critics, that he had written nonsense:

What the reader will not find in these pages is one of those uninterrupted strings of dramatic and thrilling episodes that travel writers try to present to the public as truthful descriptions. Some say that in this volume, I have accumulated enough heartrending facts, scenes of atrocious infanticides, abandonment, and cannibalism to compose five more in the style of Gustave Aymard and his ilk who publish fiction about savagery, had I even known how to write such things.[45] But the critics who gave themselves license to make such remarks have forgotten that I am a missionary who reports on his travels and not someone who makes up things for a novel. By taste and by nature, I am an enemy of fiction and have always preferred history instead. As for those who make more malicious insinuations, attempting to deny my work, my travels, and even—who would believe it?—my identity, I have no alternative but to oppose them with absolute contempt. I have enough documents in front of me to answer those envious people, and my writings will stand up to any scrutiny.[46]

He then launched an angry defense, which began with a legitimate distinction between his books and the then wildly popular novels featuring the so-called redskins of the American West (he was perhaps an "enemy of fiction," but that did not prevent him from imagining a good part of his book on the Inuit, *Les grands Esquimaux*). He continued by challenging and mocking French critics who were ignorant of any of the realities of the Canadian Far North, and ended by denouncing the malicious, vile, and envious people who tried to make him and his works disappear. As Émile Petitot penned these lines in Mareuil-lès-Meaux in 1893 for the introduction to the fourth volume of his memoirs, it appears that his feelings of generalized persecution had not weakened much in the ten years since his discharge from the mental institution in Montreal.

★

In spite of the fears and constant opposition from the Catholic hierarchy, Émile Petitot managed to get some of his works published, most often by ephemeral Parisian presses. Each volume of his memoirs was put out by a different publisher, which shuttered its business soon after the work was published. As a result, the ex-missionary seems to have had great difficulty in recuperating some of his royalties as author.[47] What his superiors feared most were possible confessions about his "special friendships" or revelations about his fears and frenzies rather than his disquisitions on the Arctic Jews—which earlier they had considered sufficiently well-founded to publish in their annals over several years. Nevertheless, a progressive distancing took place between the Oblats vis-à-vis the articles he kept on sending them. Since 1870, while encouraging him to pursue his studies, the editorial board of the annals had become more cautious:

> We are following up on a study by Reverend Petitot on the Montagnais nation. It is not up to us to make a judgment on the opinion that our dear colleague supports or on the arguments he invokes. We will only allow ourselves to encourage him in this interesting research, which he is conducting along with the most difficult work of apostolic zeal. We have noted and will continue to make note of the results of this research as valuable data that other observations may confirm or modify in the future. The reader will not lose sight of the fact that Father Petitot himself maintains a measured and critical perspective: as he says, he is not giving us a fully developed thesis that he considers indisputably proven but only a study, a series of notes that can be used to start the discussion.[48]

Seven years later, the editors were even more reserved. Although the Oblates considered Émile Petitot's impromptu presentation at the First Congress of Americanists in Nancy to be a legendary triumph, his arguments were so implacable that they undermined freethought principles of logic and empiricism.[49] The editorial comments attached to one of his articles in the annals now expressed much clearer distance with heavy innuendo.

> We are publishing the work of the Reverend Father Petitot as a document, not as a proven truth. We believe that it is useful to investigate the trace of Biblical traditions through the legends of the most remote peoples of the New World, which is why we readily applaud our laborious colleague's research. However, we leave the responsibility to him for his observations and the conclusions he draws from them. If we may voice

our opinion, it seems to us that the author pushes the efforts of harmonizing them too far. We express our full reservations about this subject, but we do not have the competence needed to make cuts in a study of this kind.[50]

Later, in a footnote to the same article, they noted,

We beg pardon from our dear colleague if we say that it does not seem possible that so many minute details of the history of the Jewish nation have been passed along and faithfully transmitted through the ages in the memory of a people in the form of fables that are so inconsistent and mixed with so many ridiculous aberrations. When ignorance and imagination are given free rein at this point, it seems difficult to us that an oral tradition would be recognizable, down to these minute details, at a distance of fifty years or fifty leagues; perhaps we would not even find two men in a tribe who report it in the same way. If this is the case, what consequence can we draw, through these kinds of minor facts, from the coincidence between the fable and history after such a considerable span of time? If the author's thesis is true—and we want to believe it—we think that tradition should be asked to give only what it can: the more or less altered memory of the most notable events.[51]

Although the thesis of the Hebrew origin of the First Nations could still be defended among ultramontane Catholics in the second half of the nineteenth century (Adrien-Gabriel Morice, another Oblate missionary, would still defend it at the beginning of the following century), it had been rejected by this time by anthropologists, philologists, and academic historians. When the editors said Émile Petitot went "too far," what they were criticizing was the priest's method. The connections were pushed too far and the historical and environmental circumstances of cultural transmission were not sufficiently taken into account. The missionary's method, under the banner of revealed truth, had gradually led to a protracted, exhaustive form of reasoning that violated all principles of common sense.

The republic of professors of the time was no more gentle with Émile Petitot's writings. After one of his lectures on the origin of First Nations peoples he delivered at a meeting of the Anthropological Society of Paris in March 1884, all the members of the academy protested "against the abusive use of etymologies to derive more or less imaginary migrations, which only leads to erroneous conclusions"—a unanimous judgment that made it clear that the former missionary was definitively expelled from the circle of duly authorized intellectuals.[52] From then on, he was completely discredited; freethought principles had taken revenge.

Four years later, Gabriel Gravier, founder of the Geographical Society of Normandy, concluded a long review of Émile Petitot's book *Les grands Esquimaux* with a brief reminder of the epistemological framework that the missionary neglected out of ignorance and ingenuousness—a framework that had become consensual in the sciences by this time—which the geographer recalled by spicing his remarks with a dose of militant atheism.

> While paleontology finds family traits between races that are far separated by space and especially by time, geology holds that we have only very confused ideas about the terrestrial revolutions of the early ages, that we know little about the geography of those distant times, and that we are in the first pages of a history about human migration. While recognizing that Mr. Petitot's works have a very real value, that they are written with talent, frankness, and good humor, we believe we must make the most express reservations concerning his insinuations about the Asian origin of the Eskimos,

insinuations that bring us back to those fanciful stories of genesis, which have always had as their supreme goal the stultification and enslavement of mankind.[53]

The reactions were similar to the publication of Émile Petitot's last book on First Nations traditions, his *Accord des mythologies dans la cosmogonie des Danites arctiques*. In *La tradition*, Henry Carnoy wrote a weary review, stating, "Father Petitot, playing with words, juggling with etymology, considers the Indians to be descendants of the Hebrews. The question of the Asian origin of the redskins can still be debated in the present state of archaeological science. But as far as their traditions are concerned, we do not see what argument can be drawn from them, since works in the field of anthropology have proved the absolute similarity of folklore among all peoples."[54] In reviewing the book for the *Revue de l'histoire des religions*, Albert Réville said it used "a general theory of mythologies that very few scholars can accept." He concluded on a bemused note: "Decidedly, the logical instrument that we use and the one played by Mr. Petitot do not make the same sounds. They were tuned to different notes, and I'm afraid we'll never be able to get them in tune with each other."[55] The reviews were thus all marked by the ironic and condescending attitude reserved for criticism of works that are easily recognized as marginal. Émile Petitot, whose amateurism and autodidactism were repeatedly noted by reviewers, was far behind the contemporary state of anthropological problems. On the Parisian scene, he had become a kind of mad scientist overtaken by the "disorders of a furibund imagination" that prevailed "to the farthest limits of an idea."[56]

★

Émile Petitot's work is nevertheless exceptional in many ways. Possessed by the furious obsession to prove the Jewish origin of the Dené, an obsession that, as we will see, led him even further into delirium, the missionary felt compelled to conduct in-depth studies of the language and oral traditions of the First Nations peoples among whom he lived. He took advantage of his initial trip back to France to supervise the publication of an enormous dictionary of Dené (*Dictionnaire de la langue dènè-dindjié*) in which he described no less than three Dené dialects (Chipewyan, Hareskin, and Kutchin) and which also contained "a large number of terms specific to seven other dialects of the same language."[57] This colossal linguistic work was made possible not only by the "truly surprising ease" with which he learned languages but also by his long, frenzied quest for Hebrew roots.

Although he was far from being the first missionary to publish a dictionary and grammar of an Indigenous language, he was far ahead of his time in publishing mythological narratives. On his own initiative, driven both by linguistic concerns and by the search for Biblical concordances, he collected narratives directly from the Dené, which he transcribed in their language and then presented in a literal interlinear translation and a literary one. The undertaking embraced many Dené storytellers, including Tsinnayé and Tsépakhé of the Yellowknives, Vitoedh and Toudhouléazé of the Kutchin, Yéttanétel and Sakranétrawotra of the Dogribs, old blind Ekounélyel of the Chipewyan, and the shaman Lizette Khatchôti of the Hareskins.[58]

Émile Petitot published this magnificent corpus in two separate books, one for philologists, financed by the Count of Charencey (one of whose first names, by a strange coincidence, was none other than Hyacinthe), the other for a cultivated readership, dedicated to the Marquise de Vatimesnil, who, it may be recalled, died in the fire of the Charity Bazaar in Paris.[59] It is true that he wrote incorrigibly that "the spirit of the Talmudists of Babylon seems to have presided over the writing of their legends," and considered the works he offered French readers to be a sort of North American Mishnah, "because of their close relationship with the books of the Hebrews."[60] Nonetheless, these works constitute, to my knowledge, the first time that an ethnographer was not content with a brief summary of the oral traditions of an Indigenous people, instead setting down the original text in all its complexity, freed as far as possible from the ideological veneer of its collector, allowing it to be endlessly retranslated, continually reinterpreted. Apart from a bibliographer who saw in him a precursor of Franz Boas, Émile Petitot's work as a transcriber and translator has almost completely fallen into oblivion.[61] I consider him to be the first ethnographer to have sufficiently raised the requirements necessary to accurately and honestly transpose an oral tradition into a written work, a minimal condition for any objective study of Indigenous knowledge.

I therefore do not hesitate to consider my own ethnographic works on Indigenous oral traditions, in particular my transcriptions and translations of shamanic incantations among the Amazonian Sharanahua, as the distant, respectful successors to his inaugural undertaking. Of course, this raises questions about the delirious, raving, and phantasmagorical origins of linguistic anthropology in general and of my work in particular.

Figure 5. Émile Petitot wearing Dené clothing in the photography studio of L. E. Desmarais in Montreal, Canada, undated (1874?). Photograph courtesy of Archives Deschâlets, Richelieu, Canada.

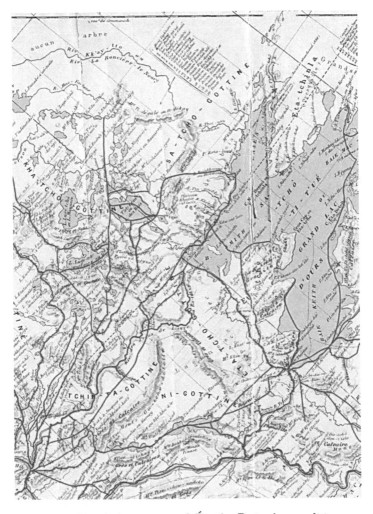

Figure 6. Detail from map of Émile Petitot's expeditions to the Inuit, 1862–1873 (based on drawing by Jules André Arthur Hansen, *Bulletin de la société de géographie* 10 [1875]). © Zones sensibles, used with permission.

CHAPTER THREE

Prophetic Frenzy
Anticipating the End Times

In the city of Amsterdam in 1644, Antonio de Montezinos, Portuguese in nationality and Jewish in religion, published a curious account that attracted the attention of a wide circle of scholars, both Jewish and Christian. While in the province of Quito during his travels in South America, he had discovered the yoke under which the Spaniards held Native peoples, who had to resign themselves to undergoing "cruel, tyrannical, and absolutely inhumane" treatment. The merchant was a Jewish converso, forced by the King of Spain to become Christian but secretly observing the law of his ancestors. He was arrested in Cartagena de Indias (now Cartagena, Colombia) by the Catholic Inquisition and thrown in prison, where he had a revelation: "These Indians are Hebrews!"[1]

As a converso, sharing a similar experience of oppression as Native peoples in the Americas must have been a major factor in this revelation. After he was released from prison, Antonio de Montezinos undertook an expedition to the forests of the Cordillera south of Cartagena (in modern-day Colombia) in search of the hidden Hebrew people. Deep in the forest, on the banks of the Magdalena River, he ended up finding a group of Indigenous people who were slightly tanned, tall, handsome, proud in bearing, with long hair sometimes reaching their knees, and who told him that, unlike the other peoples who surrounded them, they alone were the sons of Abraham, Isaac, Jacob, and Israel. The Marrano trader stayed with them for three days while they told him their story, replete with conflicts they had with Indigenous peoples and their pagan sorcerers. Once Montezinos gained their trust, they passed along a prophecy to him:

> The God of the sons of Israel is the true God and everything that is written on their tablets is the truth. At the end of time, they will be the masters of all nations. People will come to this country to bring you many gifts, and when all the land is filled with wealth, these children of Israel will leave their seclusion and become masters of the whole world, thus restoring their original sovereignty.[2]

The astonishing account of the discovery of Israelites in the Americas quickly spread through the Jewish community in Amsterdam and aroused their messianic enthusiasm. The last lost tribe had been found at last in the rainforest, and soon the Jewish people would be restored to their position as "masters of the world." Rabbi Menasseh ben Israel was asked to take a stand on the veracity of the account. After examining reports by explorers and missionaries as well as the Holy Scripture and Judaic traditions, he attested to its accuracy. In his book *The Hope of Israel*, published in 1650, he traced the migrations of the lost tribes and concluded that, if the people met by Montezinos were indeed Jewish, the other Indigenous peoples were more likely descendants of the Tartars. Unlike the belief commonly accepted by the "Spaniards who live in the West Indies," for whom all "the Indians originate from the Ten Tribes," ben Israel thus propounded a theory of a double migration to the Americas, something that was also found two centuries later among the Mormons.[3]

However, what was most significant for Menasseh ben Israel was the prediction reported by Montezinos and confirmed by many prophets of the Scriptures: the end of time was near, when the people of Israel, after much suffering, would soon be restored to their rightful place, and the twelve Hebrew tribes scattered around the world would gather under the authority of a single prince, the Messiah, son of David, who, by setting up a temporal and spiritual monarchy, would establish universal peace.[4]

This messianic hope was "the hallmark of both Menasseh's thought and life," which would unexpectedly converge with a form of Christian millenarianism that was exacerbated in the mid-eighteenth century by an apocalyptic interpretation of the comets, wars, invasions, and rebellions that seemed to be on the rise.[5] This new millenarianism, based on a particular reading of the Old Testament, specifically concerning Daniel's visions, predicted the coming of the "Fifth Monarchy" and the inevitable reign of the saints. It adopted a new attitude toward the Jewish people: they were now considered to hold the keys to the Kingdom, since the end times could not come about until they returned to the Holy Land, where they would finally all be reunited.[6]

Exchanges between Christian and Jewish scholars then took place on the basis of this common messianism, leading to renewed interest in the problem of the location of the lost tribes of Israel. Menasseh ben Israel wrote *The Hope of Israel* at the request of Protestant millenarists who had heard of Antonio de Montezinos's account—among them the Scotsman John Dury (who had determined that the end of time would take place in 1655) and the English theologian Nathaniel Homes (who supported the readmission of Jewish people into England). Ben Israel cautiously ignored his main disagreement with Christians, who considered the fall of the Antichrist and the conversion of all practitioners of Judaism to Christianity to be indispensable prerequisites for the coming of the Messiah.[7]

★

The historian Richard H. Popkin has shown how, starting from these exchanges, theories that sought to prove the Jewish origin of the contemporary Native peoples of the Americas, when scaffolded in the Christian world, became tinged with messianism. The conversion of these peoples would indeed be equivalent to the conversion of the last lost tribes of Israel, a sign that the end times were near. This messianic tone is evident in various books: Thomas Thorowgood's *Jewes in America, or Probabilities that the Americans are of that Race* (1650) in connection with the initial conversion of Indigenous peoples in New England; James Adair's *The History of the American Indians* (1775) and Elias Boudinot's *A Star in the West, or A Humble Attempt to Discover the Long Lost Ten Tribes of Israel, Preparatory to Their Return to Their Beloved City, Jerusalem* (1816) at the time of the millenarian ferment that accompanied the American Revolution; and Joseph Smith's famous *Book of Mormon* (1830) at the founding of a new religion.[8]

Even if Émile Petitot, when he developed his own theory of the Jewish origin of the Dené, knew nothing of this millenarian tradition (his few references to predecessors, all prior to Menasseh ben Israel, seem to come from a volume of Abbot Migne's 1844–1846 encyclopedia), he did not fail to comprehend the magnitude of the eschatological import of his discovery.[9] For if these remote First Nations were Jewish, which he no longer doubted, then, the missionary inferred, by translating Deuteronomy 30:4 in a rather personal way, "The conversion of the Jews would take place here without the world knowing it and the prophetic word of the holy books would be fulfilled: 'If any of thine be driven out unto the outmost parts of heaven ... from thence will the Lord thy God gather thee, and from thence will he fetch thee.'"[10] This conversion of the polar Israelites would herald a glorious future for Émile Petitot, who sometimes wondered if he himself might be "a sign of the end times."[11]

This slight uncertainty would form the touchstone of the missionary's final stage of madness: this consisted of not only his imaginary persecutions and exorbitant theory of the Hebrew origin of the Dené but also a personal messianism through which, during his violent episodes of schizoid rage, he became at once Jewish, Indigenous, and prophet.

★

In the nineteenth century, messianism was common in Canada's Far North. The Dené, who discovered Christianity at the same time as they were decimated by rampant epidemics, saw many prophets appear in their midst, all promising them redemption in a better world to come.[12] The Oblate missionary Vital Grandin was the first to recount his encounter with one of these prophets in 1858 among the Dené Chippewayans:

One fine morning, a young savage from Île-à-la-Crosse was overcome by a strong inspiration. From then on, he was no longer a man like any other; from the moment he was no longer a man, given that progress does not allow descent, he had to be a god. Yes, none other than "the Son of God" was on earth. This new deification of the man, as in all the other cases, led to the rejection of prayer, the Gospel, in a word, of everything that reminds us of our own humility and the greatness of the Creator of all things. But he was a madman! Yes, undoubtedly, as are all those who push their poor reasoning toward spheres where the one who created them does not allow them to reach. However, since many madmen form schools, it is not surprising that ours found followers. He was taken at his word by those who were seduced by a certain verbiage he adopted, which neither he nor the others understood. He did wonders; at least he did one that was astonishing to us who know the Montagnais: he ordered his followers to get rid of everything they owned. To be more worthy to walk in the company of the "Son of God," they destroyed or burned everything they had, and soon the entire nation was upended.[13]

Noting that the Dené were deserting his mission, Vital Grandin went once again to the village of the Son of God:

This purported god ruled over his whole band, which feared him, convinced that he was possessed of a spirit superior to that of man. According to what his followers said, he spoke all languages and performed miracles. I had no trouble recognizing a madman and his type of vainglorious hallucination. He called out to me as soon as I was within reach, "Come, my son, I will show you wonders, you will see the tablets of Moses!" At every moment, he kept repeating, "Theos, Theos!" I wondered where he could have learned a Greek word. He held in his hands pieces of aspen bark six feet long and as wide as his hand. Then he tried to knock me out with this bark, hitting me on the head wherever he could catch me, so I had to throw myself into my canoe with two of my men to get away. The mother of the new god, as mad as the god himself, threw herself into the icy water up to her waist and held onto my canoe: "Why are you afraid?" she cried. "He didn't hit you in order to hurt you, he did it so you could share in his spirit!"[14]

A few years later, Émile Petitot, who had just arrived in the missions of boreal Canada, made a short stopover at a village of the same people, where all that remained was the memory of the prophet:

At the far side of the lake, we stopped at a village of Christian Chippewayans to administer to a dying man. These Dené had just gone through a schism that almost turned their poor heads inside out. Its author was a mad theomaniac who presented himself to his compatriots as the reincarnated Jesus Christ. His Indian name was

Inazè, Little Dog, a pure savage. He then began calling himself the Son of God. These weak-brained savages fell right into the trap and began to adore the hoaxer. Taking advantage of his followers' simplicity, Little Dog Son of God tried to persuade them that he had the power, if he wanted, to turn them into beasts. "Khou, Khou," he often said to his favorite disciple, Khatarré, Hareskin Lining, almost as crazy as he. "Khou, come on, come on, you're almost transformed into a bear! Now crawl on all fours and growl like one," added the lunatic. "That's it, there you go! A few more days of practice and your transformation will be complete."

One day, Little Dog decided to get rid of his clothes and don a heavenly garment. All madmen have similar whims. He even persuaded his sectarians to do the same. "The kingdom of God has come," he told them. "We will recover our original innocence and be like Adam and Eve in the garden of delights. So, quickly, let's get rid of everything we got from those depraved people!" And he served as an example. Immediately the Chippewayans lit a bonfire and threw not only their clothes but also their utensils and even their weapons into it. Then they piously walked through the groves like Adam and Eve, waiting for the promises of the reincarnated Son of God to be fulfilled.[15]

Émile Petitot concluded this supposedly edifying story with a striking reference to the Mormons, with whom he shared a similar conception of the Jewish origin of certain Indigenous populations:

It would be difficult to believe and understand such an aberration if history did not teach us that many European peoples have gone through the same phase of religious lunacy that produced the Adamites, the Poor Men, the Flagellants, and the Anabaptists, and if we did not still see the same madmen imposing themselves on the gullible crowd and drawing followers calling themselves Mormons, Shakers, Quakers, Free-Lovers, and Spiritists.[16]

Two years later, in 1864, Émile Petitot wrote in his letters, with the usual mocking condescension, about a new messianic movement that appeared among the Dené Dogribs of the Rae Lakes, specifically among five of their shamans (called *inkranzé* in their language):

The profligacy of the imagination of these poor savages, combined with their natural love for religion, or rather, for everything that belongs to the supernatural order, was bound to lead some of them to mysticism and madness, and that is what happened. Yes, these ignorant Indians, who are still catechumens, have already seen the rise of Nicolas and Marcion, who, like the first proponents of heresies, heeding only their mad pride and putting full faith in their bizarre and ridiculous dreams, imagine themselves to be priests and inspired by God. A similar thing happened to the Gwich'in at Fort MacPherson, but a minister was there who was careful not to contradict and condemn them.

I could not do the same with the five visionaries— four men and an old woman—whom I met among the Dogribs. They had already expressed the wish to their compatriots that I would recognize them as priests and allow them to continue with their sacrilegious farces. One of them, not as bad as the others, came to explain his doctrine to me, which he said he got from God Himself. While preserving their belief in the Holy Trinity, Jesus Christ, the Blessed Virgin, and the saints, he nevertheless denied Communion and Mass and promised three heavens, depending on the degree of holiness of each person: a black heaven for common saints, a gray one for those of greater holiness, and a white one for those who would be allowed to see God. These "Godly people" had replaced our hymns with a kind of monotonous song composed of two syllables, which they said had been revealed to a sick person by the good Lord.

On Sunday, May 22, the four madmen gathered most of the tribe on a hill overlooking the camp, where they had set up a *chounsh* or *inkranzé* lodge. Then they gave themselves free rein to repeating their previous circus acts. Warned by one of my neophytes, I went to the scene and observed all the infidel savages sitting on their heels in front of the mound where the four *inkranzé* were located. They sang as they swayed back and forth like idiots. Suddenly the most fanatical circus performer rose and gave me a glaring look.... "You, who are you to oppose our designs? What is your power? Where is your potency, you who confess to not see God and to not receive any revelation from Him? As for me, I see Him, God, and I speak with Him face to face. So stop acting like the master here and go back to where you came from! We don't need you here!"[17]

Émile Petitot said he had observed similar prophets "in each tribe" he had visited.[18] The Dené, at a critical juncture in their history, thus appropriated some of the elements of the Christian missionaries' religion, which their shamans adapted to their traditional beliefs and then proposed a new formula to their people. By means of a bricolage of ceremonies, among which were strange forms of baptism, books made of bark, collective lodges, half-Catholic half-shamanic psalmodies, and ritual dances, the shamans became the prophets of a new god (to whom missionaries had access only through the Bible) and promised a better world without epidemics or dependence on manufactured goods, a "kingdom of God," a kind of three-tiered paradise.[19] Émile Petitot was thus surrounded by Dené messiahs who constantly reminded him of the imminence of the end of the world.[20]

No doubt these messianic eruptions among the Dené peoples, whom he considered to be the last descendants of the tribe of the Danites (the group from which, according to some Church Fathers, the Antichrist would arise), must have perturbed the anxious spirit of the missionary. Yet he spoke of the Dené prophets only with condescension and irony, considering them more as competitors than as divine signs. Twenty-five years later, in the second volume of *Mémoires d'un missionaire*, he resumed his description of the Dogrib prophets, adding that they were "mad theomaniacs" and that their dances and songs were "worthy of an insane asylum," which resonated with his description of Little Dog Son of God as a "theomaniac," a "maniac," and a "lunatic."[21] This use of a stigmatizing vocabulary of pathology was common among missionaries at the time—Vital Grandin described Little Dog Son of God as "mad" and "hallucinated"—but Émile Petitot used more technical terms taken directly from the lexicon of the alienists of the time, particularly after his stay in France from 1874 to 1876.

This was the same time that he began to use psychiatric terms to describe certain Dené customs. For instance, he now said shamans were affected by a "cervical lesion."

> Tåhchyé himself and his old wife ended up asking me to baptize them. I gave this patriarch the name Abraham, and his wife, Sarah. May God reward this poor fool for his faith and charity. However, baptism could not cure him of his hallucinations or, more precisely, his obsessions. There are some hopeless cases in the world. For that poor, aching shamanic brain, it was a matter of routine. The pattern was set: his habit of seeing the devil was fixed, his imagination atrophied, with bats in the belfry, the building haunted, bewitched, beyond repair. It's a pity, but the psychological fact is understandable. It is so closely linked and dependent on the cervical lesion that, if it is not healed, there is no hope of modifying it.[22]

The dances of the Dené reminded Émile Petitot of the exercises practiced in the "insane asylums," institutions that, after his stay at Longue Pointe Asylum in Montreal, he could talk about with all the authority of experience.

> I was hoping that after they had skipped around in circles for a couple of hours—an exercise that would be very popular and entertaining in Bicêtre or Charenton—my neophytes would have had enough of this virtuous, heroic fun and would hurry to bed. But this was not the case. I realized that at the end of the Last Steppe of Great Bear Lake, as at the Paris Opera, it is easier to get dancers moving, especially the women, than to stop their legs once they have begun. No matter how monotonous and macabre for my taste the tunes were that they hooted to me in unison; no matter how supremely boring their single-file whirling was, my good Danites found such great artistic delight in them that I did not have the heart to interrupt such innocent and well-performed entertainment and extinguish the fires of concupiscence forever.[23]

This strange pathologizing of Dené culture was most likely connected to Émile Petitot's own psychiatric consultations. Even if he never considered the constant persecution he perceived from those around him to be "imaginary fears," he did worry about the attacks of mania that carried him away at regular intervals and left him exhausted. In July 1869, after one of his most violent crises, he wrote a letter to his superior, saying, "I am still waiting impatiently for the reports of the doctor in Paris, the doctor at Fort Simpson having admitted to me that he does not understand anything about my infirmity."[24] We know that he took advantage of his stay in France to consult alienists, perhaps even his cousin Prosper Despine, the most famous psychiatric doctor in Marseilles. While reading Prosper Despine's books, Émile Petitot would have found an abundance of terms derived from the psychiatrist

Jean-Étienne Dominique Esquirol, from "cervical lesions" to "theomania," the latter being defined as follows:

> Theomania is about ideas that relate to the supreme being, angels, mysticism, miracles, predictions of future events. Theomaniacs always believe they are prophets; it is God who speaks through their mouths; they claim to be able to reform religions and perform miracles. These fanatics have hallucinations, delusions, and visions related to their delirious ideas, phenomena that confirm them in their ideas.[25]

However, Émile Petitot was not satisfied with more or less metaphorically describing Dené messiahs as theomaniacs, their shamans as hallucinators suffering from cervical lesions, or their dances as insane asylum exercises. He also described what he considered to be cultural syndromes, mental illnesses specific to First Nations peoples:

> When I examine the caliber and temperament of the redskins' character and weigh the value and strength of some of their reasoning, I cannot help but notice that many of these people are simply insane or monomaniacs. Who knows, perhaps the nomadic savage life has had, from its beginning, no other principle, no other impulse than madness and hallucination, which leads unfortunate people to flee the society of sane people to join like-minded company.[26]

Despite the use of Esquirol's vocabulary (such as "monomania"), perhaps resulting from discussions with Prosper Despine or from reading his books, Émile Petitot's assessment continued in these overly broad terms, but he soon made it clear:

> The fundamentally timid character of the Dené makes them constantly see enemies where there is no shadow

of them. They always imagine they are surrounded by obstacles, offended, attacked, oppressed, and pursued by bitter enemies. They all have persecution mania. I will be told that it is an unfortunate relic of old internal quarrels between tribes, that it is the result of their miserable kind of life, living alone, lost in the middle of the woods, fleeing in some way the society of their fellow men, that it is most probably the consequence of their immigration to these terrible wastelands. I accept all these reasons, but nonetheless, I observe that the Danite nation is riven as a whole with persecution mania.[27]

It is hard to believe: the missionary projected onto the Dené a "persecution mania" from which he, having immigrated to the hostile territories of the Far North, was the first to be affected. But now that he had started down such a fruitful path, he was not about to stop. He elaborated:

There are no idiots among them, nor, strictly speaking, any madmen; but there are many hallucinators and monomaniacs. Whatever the cause, this nervous overexcitability disturbs their bodies so much that it causes them to lose the self-control that redskins normally exercise; but the worst thing is that this morbid condition of their imagination sympathetically affects all their neighbors. We have seen many cases of these contagious fits of temporary madness in all the tribes and at all latitudes. The pagan women are especially prone to them. In some cases, the hallucination of one or two visionaries won over the entire tribe to such an extent that it carried them into the most extravagant acts. Every year during the summer, fear also spreads among them irrationally like an epidemic. They then live in continuous trances and in fear of an imaginary enemy who incessantly pursues them and whom they believe they see everywhere, even though he exists nowhere.[28]

The Dené, "riven as a whole with persecution mania," were thus subject to attacks of madness when they—especially the women, as Émile Petitot commented—lost "control of themselves." The priest was referring here to what ethnographic and then psychiatric literature in the twentieth century came to call "Arctic hysteria," sometimes referred to by its Inuktitut name, *pibloktoq*. A few decades later, another Oblate missionary described one of the first known examples:

> One day we were called to help a young person who, following a nervous shock in a mental depression, suffered a first attack and then two more acute ones. She screamed, panted, moaned, and wheezed as she breathed with difficulty. For a moment, her body was shaking, her hands and arms contorting. Then, after a spasm, she became almost completely unresponsive. Finally, when she revived, she was in a daze, her head aching, in a stupor.[29]

Attacks of Arctic hysteria sometimes became more violent. In the 1950s, an anthropologist collected evidence of this from the Inuit of Iglulik.

> Everyone was sitting on the *illeq* (the igloo platform); Aggiaq's mother began to puff and pant, with her eyes "bulging and incandescent," he explained. Then she got up, headed for the kayak, beating the snow in the air for a long time, one fist after another. Half squatting, she puffed like the wind: pfffff! On the *illeq*, the assistants were terrified. Half naked, she reached the ice floe, screaming at the top of her lungs.[30]

These fits of "hysterical" frenzy that seized mostly women were very similar to Émile Petitot's crises, his "attacks of nervous fever followed by delirium," his "waking dreams so painful and deceptive that they quite resemble madness."[31]

Jean Séguin, his colleague at the Good Hope Mission, described a particularly violent episode at the end of the winter of 1869, when Émile Petitot became "raving mad for six days."[32]

> Every day, he had three fits of frenzy, one during the day and the others at night, one around midnight and the other around five or six o'clock in the morning. Last night, I thought he was possessed by the devil. He no longer listened to anything; he ran away, despite our efforts, into a terrible wind and cold of 36 degrees below. Hiding outside, he took off his shirt and cassock. We brought him in half frozen, but he still wanted to escape. I gave him another good thrashing, after which I only had to talk to keep him quiet. Everyone at the fort was afraid, and my assistants had no courage to spare.[33]

Like the Dené and Inuit, Émile Petitot entered an uncontrollable trance on these occasions and, despite the cold, tried to get rid of his clothes; as he would say knowingly, "all madmen have similar whims." Then, continued Jean Séguin, "he made sharp and piercing cries, like those who are in this state do, and looked at me with flaming eyes," once again like the Dené "monomaniacs" and other "theomaniacs" Émile Petitot described.[34] At the end of these bouts, he remembered nothing but having been seriously ill. To learn what happened, he sometimes unsealed letters written by his colleagues and read their accounts of his madness and the treatment to which he had been subjected.[35] There is no doubt that the missionary's crises were similar to attacks of Arctic hysteria.

However, Émile Petitot insisted that the cases of "temporary madness" he had observed among the Indigenous peoples he knew were transmitted "by contagion" or in an "epidemic manner," which may seem surprising. By claiming that most of the Dené, in the final analysis, were suffering from monomania, he was apparently mixing together attacks of hysteria, persecution mania, and messianic movements. Or is it better to view this amalgam and these terms as an echo of Prosper Despine's ideas? Indeed, the Marseilles alienist, once again following Esquirol, believed that forms of "epidemic madness" existed, which propagated through "moral contagion," among them being theomania and states of hysteria.[36] Émile Petitot was certainly familiar with his cousin's ideas, which were published in 1875 in a tome of over a thousand pages and which had a decisive influence on the former's interpretation of Dené culture. From this perspective, it is striking to realize that, in the midst of his outpouring of partial projections, the notion of moral contagion probably applied above all to Émile Petitot himself. He may have been the first Westerner to be infected with the attacks of mania typical of Arctic hysteria or even the theomania of messianic movements. Going mad also meant going native.

★

Émile Petitot's fits of madness were indeed characterized by religious and messianic delirium, leading him to develop certain views about Arctic Jews to their most extreme form, constantly revolving around a few fixed ideas: circumcision, the Antichrist, and the end of the world. On August 18, 1869, for example, after a major crisis, Émile Petitot sent an enthusiastic letter to Laurent-Achille Rey:

> Do you perhaps remember what I once told you about the striking similarities between Jewish observances and Dené customs? My vague opinion is confirmed by what I have just read in the report of Mackenzie's discovery of the Mackenzie River in 1700 and more, namely, "that he believed he recognized in many Indians, Slavey, and Hareskins the marks of circumcision." If the fact is true, it corroborates everything I had the honor of writing to you about this chapter in the past; and one could not

help but draw the conclusion that the redskins, if not actually Jews, at least knew the Mosaic Law.[37]

Émile Petitot had been living in Canada's Far North for seven years and his relationship with Native peoples was sometimes intimate. Nevertheless, it was in the report of a Scottish explorer that he learned of the alleged existence of this Jewish custom: "Whether circumcision be practiced among them, I cannot pretend to say, but the appearance of it was general among those whom I saw."[38]

The tone of Alexander Mackenzie's statement was hardly assertive (what had he really seen, after all?), but Émile Petitot immediately saw it as the keystone of the argument he had been building for several years. A year later, in another letter to Laurent-Achille Rey, when he once again went over the supposedly analogous traditions of the Hebrews and Dené, the circumcision of the latter had become a certainty for him:

> It is not only the Dené and Dindjié traditions that provide the proofs I am talking about; there is one stronger than all the others, and that is the near universal practice of circumcision on the eighth day. The Reverend Father Séguin and I have no more doubts: the Kutchin, Hareskins, the Indians of the Rocky Mountains, Bear Lake, etc., are all circumcised; we know from Alexander Mackenzie that the Slavey are too. It remains to be seen whether the Dogribs, Castors, and Montagnais are as well. But since they are Indians belonging to the same language, it is probable that they do. If you add to this the fact that the Dené perform a ceremony exactly like the Jewish Passover ... I have no doubt that you will be astonished and tempted to truly view our Dené as Jews. As for me, I have no further doubts.[39]

The supposed ubiquity of circumcision among the Dené thus definitively convinced the missionary. He was nevertheless more cautious when, at the Nancy Congress of Americanists, he presented this discovery to an audience of scholars and learned professors:

> In many of the northernmost tribes of the Dené-Dindjié nation, male circumcision has been and perhaps still is practiced. I say perhaps, since we have not yet interfered with this custom, about which our savages do not speak openly.[40]

The Dené "concealed" this practice from Émile Petitot, stimulating both his curiosity and his imagination. That is why he rejoiced when Lizette Khatchoti Hareskin told him about an ancient practice ("before the French arrived in our country") that he immediately assimilated to circumcision:

> As soon as the newborn child became a little strong and his face turned a little crimson, the following was done to prevent the condition called "tremors": the skin of the penis was cut off with a sharp stone, and then, with the help of an awl, his cheeks and arms, earlobe and septum of the nose were pierced. Finally, with the same awl, a little blood was drawn from the palms of his hands and the soles of his feet.[41]

It is worth citing Petitot's literal translation of this tradition:

> The little boys are born, so when a little strong they have become, their face has crimson become, the trembling against their penis skin, a slice is made a flint with. Then an awl with their arms too, their cheeks too were pierced, their ears too, their nose cartilage also was pierced.[42]

Obliged to mirror the original Dené text, Émile Petitot had to split off a footnote to explain his translation of the term "penis skin" (*ekwéwèh*):

Since circumcision is something held in secret among the Dené, this word is subject to ambiguity. Indeed, ékwéwè is the name of the navel and ékwè is one of the names of the virile parts; adding the word skin, éwéh, creates the word ékwé-wèh. In this way, the operation can be disguised within earshot of laypersons. I know for certain that some priests were outraged by this ceremony, so the Indians told them that it only involved the navel.[43]

The evidence given by the missionary was thus ambiguous, at the very least: a more economical and obvious interpretation would be to view it as dealing with only the section of the umbilical cord or what remains of it a few days after the birth. But Émile Petitot was absolutely intent on believing these First Nations peoples were circumcised. Among the Dindjié (the Loucheux or Kutchin), he even discovered, or rather fantasized, the practice of adult circumcision:

The Dindjié amount to no more than 2,000 souls. The number of uncircumcised people is very small among them, I was assured. They perform this operation, like the Dené Hareskins, using a sharp flint. Some Dindjié told me that an adult who has not been circumcised after birth should perform this operation himself without receiving help from a third party, something I consider to be a very harsh and cruel ordeal.[44]

Is it necessary to point out that, apart from Alexander Mackenzie's vague account, no other missionary, ethnographer, or traveler reported a similar custom among the Dené? The opinion of Émile Grouard, a great friend of Émile Petitot who arrived in Canada on the same boat, became a bishop and lived sixty-nine years in the Far North, is clear on this point:

As for circumcision, which Father Petitot said was practiced among the Hareskins, I replied that I had never heard of it among the Slavey of the Mackenzie, nor among the Yellowknives of Great Slave Lake, nor among the Montagnais of Lake Athabaska.[45]

Circumcision obsessed Émile Petitot for a long time. In a letter Jean Séguin wrote to his bishop, in which once again his deep exasperation is palpable ("supposing that Your Holiness is as tired as I am with this chapter"), he recounted how his colleague, during a new episode of mania that lasted several days, put his obsession into action:

He tried and perhaps succeeded in circumcising himself during his madness, since circumcision, according to him, was obligatory. One day, he was looking for something on the floor, saying, "Did you see the piece? I don't know what I did with it." As he said this, he pulled his hand out from under his cassock and it was all bloody. I asked what the blood was from, and instead of answering me, he punched me in the face. Since he was always talking about the obligation of circumcision, I conclude that he had done it to himself.[46]

Émile Petitot had thus apparently inflicted "a very harsh and cruel ordeal on himself," and Jean Séguin remained on the alert from then on:

Circumcision continues to cause him great torment, and every day I have to take some new sharp tool out of his hands. He collected a supply of them, which he hid under his bed and which I found after searching everywhere.[47]

Three years later, when he returned from his stay in France, his episodes of mania resumed. "He was bereft of all reason for ten days," wrote Jean Séguin, who then gingerly described his colleague's behavior:

Circumcision was absolutely necessary and he had to perform it on himself as a matter of utmost necessity. Although he is never left alone day or night, I have a strong suspicion that he did something to himself because I found a razor with blood on it on his table one day. I asked him the reason why, but he wouldn't answer me.[48]

The following year, Séguin wrote:

He had nothing but circumcision on his mind and did everything in his power to get it done. He tried it himself but he couldn't; he asked me; he asked the brother; since his request was badly received, he asked people at the fort, who refused to do it; then the Indians; after the adults refused, he turned to the young people and forced three or four of them to cut some pieces for him. They told him that they did not want to, that it was a sin, but he told them that it was good, that it was necessary.[49]

That same year, Jean Séguin saw Émile Petitot come back from an expedition to the Dené with a pale complexion, a distraught face, and a sick and tired look. The priest, with his hands gripping his lower abdomen, told him, "I have just cut another piece of myself for these people (speaking of the young people), and I think I cut an artery because it won't stop bleeding."[50] He was unable to walk for five or six days.

A few months later, Jean Séguin, now thoroughly wearied, reported:

The Reverend Father Petitot fell back into his old mental aberrations during the summer by getting himself circumcised by the savages who worked at the mission, because he had heard from the Gwich'in, when they passed by on the barges, that if he was not circumcised when they returned, they would put him to death.[51]

Self-mutilation was now explicitly linked to his delusions of persecution. Around this same time, another Oblate missionary, Auguste Lecorre, who had recently arrived in the Far North and was assigned to the mission at Fort Providence, offered quite precise testimony on the missionary's erratic behavior:

The Reverend Father Petitot came to us from Good Hope in September, as mentally ill as ever. The Reverend Father Séguin, who brought him here and whom I have not had the pleasure of seeing again, will tell you what it is about. The poor invalid himself, who has never been as well as today, from what he told me, will not fail to tell you about his monomania. In summary, here is what I gathered from the interviews I had with him on three different occasions:

"For a long time," he told me, "I heard the Gwich'in and even the Hareskins say, 'Oh, he's a dog! He hasn't given us anything of himself; he doesn't listen to us when we tell him, "Give me something from your mittens, a little piece of your sleeve."' I was unable to understand for a long time; finally, I thought I grasped the meaning of all this: they were asking me for a piece of my flesh; it was about circumcision. The last time I was among the Gwich'in, I heard them clearly threaten to kill me if I didn't do that. 'Because he doesn't want to give himself to us and be like us, he must die like the dog that he is!' But I didn't have the courage to do the operation myself, yet I would be willing to have the four veins opened to prove to them that I love them. So I asked a Gwich'in to do it to me. He gave me the little piece of flesh he cut off, and I asked him what I should do with it. 'You should throw it away,' he told me. I thought it was over at that point, but after a while, I heard the same things again: 'He's bourgeois, he doesn't want to do anything.' I decided to get circumcised twice more since then and I asked twice again what to do with the piece: 'It gets thrown away,' I was always told. I thought that after having sacrificed myself this way three times, I would be regarded as one of them, but not at all; I still hear the same stories I've heard ever since I arrived here. What can I do? Look at my hair and beard, Father, how white they have become after all my worries over the past year! It's as if I were in a dream. Father Séguin, to whom I confided my sorrows, called all this madness and threatened to forbid me to attend Mass if I didn't abandon these ideas.

"And now, Father, tell me what you think: I still have a little bit of the corona left. If I have to give it, I must find enough charity from one of my brothers to do this to me and finally put myself on the right path. On my own, I tell you quite frankly, I don't feel brave enough to take a knife and do the operation on myself. Moreover, I do not believe I am violating my vow of chastity this way."

Imagine, Your Excellency, my astonishment and embarrassment! Trying to dissuade him by repeating that all this is madness was a useless effort. I know from experience after a year spent in Good Hope that monomania cannot be cured through reasoning.[52]

Émile Petitot's obsession with circumcision had several different aspects that I think should be clearly distinguished. First of all, it is quite likely that taking such actions was for him a way of repressing persistent and forbidden homosexual desires or even atoning for what he considered to be a serious fault, which had become notorious (he said that the Dené called him a dog, which according to him, they considered the paragon of the sodomite).[53] Thus, circumcision would have been, for him, an attenuated form of castration, an extreme solution found in some famous cases of paranoia. I am thinking in particular of William

Chester Minor, a doctor who was a contemporary of the missionary and who shared a similar fate in many ways. He was a confirmed bachelor, locked up in a British asylum as early as 1872 for murdering a worker who, he believed, was persecuting him, just as he believed that men persecuted him every night by breaking into his room to sodomize and torture him or taking him to brothels where they forced him to abuse young boys. During his confinement, William Chester Minor became one of the most prolific lexicographers of the magnificent Oxford dictionary. More radically, he also ended up cutting off his penis.[54] The case of Émile Petitot may therefore represent a variation of the same syndrome suffered by the English lexicographer.

Perhaps as an analogous form of painful and atonement directed against his sexual orientation, Émile Petitot forced himself into a strange "spiritual marriage" with a Métis woman, Marguerite Nikamous, with whom he lived for a month before being locked up in Longue Pointe Asylum.[55] The bishop who had Émile Petitot interned in fact perceived a continuity between the deeds of circumcision, castration (although the priest never seems to have gone this far except in the bishop's imagination), and his marriage: "Our poor patient had already attested on the Mackenzie of his desire to marry. He was convinced that the Montagnais were complaining about him because he was lacking something. In order to be acceptable to them, he wanted to try circumcision and castration, and now he is trying a third remedy," that is, marriage. Émile Petitot's sexual self-mutilation and, secondarily, his unusual marriage should therefore be considered as excessive forms of penance, attempts to make it impossible to act on his homosexuality, which he experienced as humiliating and unholy.[56]

However, his repeated circumcisions were more than that. They were also part of the delirious interpretions the priest developed around his notion of Jewish Indians. He convinced himself of the need for circumcision to meet the expectations of the Dené (both Hareskins and Kutchin) and, in the same way, forced their myths into his interpretation, transforming an umbilical cord into a foreskin and hearing allusions to circumcision in their most innocuous remarks. Thus, according to the missionary François-Xavier Ducot, who arrived later at Our Lady of Good Hope Mission,

> The Reverend Father constantly hears the savages say in covert terms that he must be circumcised! He keeps hearing them say to each other, "Why doesn't he do it? Ah, he's not one of us yet. He doesn't want to do it. If he doesn't do it by the time the barges come, he'll see what happens. . . ." He claims to hear even small children of five or six years old making this last threat to him. He even claims that the savages have insulted him by saying, "You fool! You don't understand that this is about you," always making allusions to circumcision.[57]

Jean Séguin went further: "They didn't speak to him clearly but they sometimes gave him signs that meant he had to circumcise himself."[58]

His acts of mutilation were therefore also a way of obeying the Hareskins and Kutchin to protect himself from their threats, certainly, but also to give himself entirely to them. Moreover, according to the testimony of one of his Oblate colleagues, Zéphyrin Gascon, the missionary sometimes insisted on distributing pieces of his severed foreskin to local Indigenous individuals, especially to the Dené wives of Métis workers, thus celebrating a somewhat perverted variant of a shamanic Eucharist.

> He thought he had to give the piece of flesh he had cut off from his genitalia, first to Lépinet's wife, who refused it indignantly, then to Nom's poor wife, who did not know what it was; she applied it as he told her on her side to get cured of her illness. Then, as it began to rot and stink, it had to be thrown away; finally, a piece was saved for the Kutchin woman. The dear father regards everything that has happened as an act of virtue and

devotion! He thinks he has given with his body what was asked of him.[59]

The missionary's circumcisions were thus endowed with an undeniably more positive aspect. Émile Petitot wanted to be accepted by the Dené at all costs; he wanted to be "looked upon as one of their own," and to him, circumcising himself or being circumcised by them meant, once again, becoming Indigenous. In doing so, it was above all his deluded theory of the Jewish origins of the Dené that he applied when he mutilated himself or asked others to mutilate him. In his eyes, circumcision transformed him into both a Dené and a Hebrew—in short, a Jew from the North Pole. The unconscious does not get delusional about the father or even the name of the father; rather, it gets delusional about ethnicities, peoples, continents, history, and geography— always a social field.

★

Émile Petitot's attacks of madness at night were always accompanied by astonishing celestial phenomena. Around ten-thirty, the faint daylight disappeared as the moon began to shine. A luminous zone appeared in the sky in the shape of a half-circle running east to west. It soon took on a strong intensity at the zenith and then suddenly turned into a nucleus of light of indescribable vividness. This erupted in movements like a multitude of lightning bolts flashing in all directions or like the spurts of colored flames when fireworks burst but on a grander scale. The colors were variegated, but most often sapphire blue dominated, a symbol of the Danite tribe, as well as a celestial white with gleaming diamonds. This electrical turmoil, like an orgasm, lasted only eight to ten seconds. When it was over, fiery lines resembling heated steel rods radiated out from the incandescent nucleus. They scattered to the edges of the far horizon, gradually fading away. Everything paused for a moment until the bright belt appeared again, much further north, and began to slowly undulate, spreading out its iridescent fringes. Almost every night, Émile Petitot, whether delirious or not, frenzied or not, contemplated these northern lights with delight.[60] The Dené considered them to be the Heart of Nature and the Spirit of Death, which "drive people's minds mad and strike them down."[61]

★

On March 6, 1876, Drs. Howard and Perrault admitted Louis Riel to the Longue Pointe mental institution in Montreal. At the age of thirty-two, the new internee refused to give his name, saying that he had been switched as a baby and put in the cradle of the real Louis Riel. He claimed that he was actually a Jew born on the beach of Marseilles and separated from his relatives. Perrault thought his madness was feigned; Howard considered him "mad because of a teratological defect in his psychophysical organization"; however, they registered him with the diagnosis of "delusions of grandeur."[62]

The patient, a French-Canadian Métis, was famous for having led the Red River Métis revolt against the Ottawa government in 1869.[63] As a fugitive from the Canadian army and militias, he had been living in exile in the United States since 1870, where he was constantly on the move, the victim of his reputation as a revolutionary, fleeing from real and imaginary enemies who all planned to murder him. In December 1875, alone on a mountaintop near Washington, he was visited by the Holy Spirit, the same one that had appeared to Moses in the midst of the flaming clouds. It filled his soul with light and carried him to the fourth heaven, where it instructed him about the nations of the earth, revealing that "the savages of North America are Jews, of the purest blood of Abraham," and declared him prophet of the New World. His mission was to save humanity by freeing it from the temporal and spiritual yoke that enslaved it. He received this divine message with his arms upraised and his head bent.

From then on, his friends feared for his mental health. He cried out all night long, constantly trying to escape and tearing up his clothes. During his violent outbursts, he shouted that he was a prophet, king, pontiff, or messiah and that he had to accomplish his mission. They took him in secret to the Montreal mental institution for his own protection and registered him under an assumed name. Monsignor Taché, the Archbishop of Red River, looked kindly on this man, whom he had seen grow up, saying "the unfortunate chief of the Métis was in the grip of megalomania and theomania."[64] But Bishop Vital Grandin, who refused to express solidarity with any revolutionaries anywhere in the world, mercilessly called Louis Riel a "miserable maniac."[65] This was the same Grandin who, in 1882, had Émile Petitot committed to the same institution near Montreal.

The delirious thinking of Louis Riel and Émile Petitot contained surprisingly similar elements: fears of being persecuted, a belief in the Jewish origin of the certain First Nations, and messianic ideas about the imminent salvation of humanity. During their episodes of mania, both of them would scream and tear off their clothes, and both considered themselves Jewish prophets. However, they were opposites in the same way a politician contrasts with a scholar. Louis Riel would go on to lead a new rebellion some ten years after his internment, during which the Métis joined First Nations peoples in an attempt to establish a new form of theocracy. But even if all those who are mad are in some way dissidents, even if "all delusion is a political statement," Émile Petitot would confine himself to writing copious studies of geography, linguistics, and folklore to prove the accuracy of his views.[66] They also opposed each other on the status they conferred on their messianic conceptions: for if Louis Riel always remained convinced of the authenticity of his divine revelation, the salvation of humanity obsessed

Émile Petitot only during his attacks of mania, which he himself acknowledged afterward were delirious. During such attacks, as we saw, he thought that the conversion of the remaining Jews, those of the North Pole, was underway, which he took as an unmistakable sign of the imminence of the end of the world, the return of Christ, and the establishment of his Kingdom.

In Biblical eschatology, however, the Second Coming is preceded by the reign of the Antichrist. This notion became a new obsession for the missionary, which may throw a different light on his identification of the Dené, the "Arctic Danites," with the descendants of the Jewish tribe of Dan-ben-Yacoub:

> Using what I already know about their eminently Hebrew practices and customs, I do not hesitate to consider the American Dané or Dené to be the sons of Dan-ben-Yacoub, the Danites. I hear a universal concert of protest. . . . It is above all fearful Christians imbued with apocalyptic ideas who will pounce on this. "Invoke Dan? The poor man, he isn't thinking straight! He must be silenced at all costs. Dan! But he is the Antichrist. Dan must come from the north and so must the Antichrist. Dan is a snake in Jacob's own testimony: 'Dan shall be a serpent by the way, an adder in the path, that biteth the horse heels, so that his rider shall fall backward.' And so, you see, this man is dangerous. He is predicting oracles. He is a converted Jew or a Jewish Christian, a false brother, an enemy of the Church," et cetera, et cetera.[67]

The voices that Émile Petitot gathered together in this paragraph are difficult to disentangle. The Dené were the descendants of a tribe of Israel, specifically the Danites, that is, the tribe of the Antichrist, according to one possible but unusual interpretation of Genesis (49:17) and Revelation (7:4). It was therefore from the Danites that "the Antichrist will emerge who will destroy and change the order of the world and nature, and who will rise above all that is God."[68] Should the Antichrist thus be sought among the First Nations, more precisely among the Dené messiahs, those "false prophets" who appeared at regular intervals in the Far North to haunt the mental landscape of the persecuted priest?

It appears that Émile Petitot never accepted this hypothesis; in the passage quoted above, he evokes this theory only to make fun of it by putting it in the mouths of "fearful Christians, imbued with apocalyptic ideas." They were implicitly embodied by the Protestant missionaries of the Far North, like William West Kirkby, Robert McDonald, or William Carpenter Bompas, the enemies of the Catholics in these lands for harvesting Native souls. In open conflict, the latter did not hesitate to consider the Oblate missionaries as representatives of the Antichrist, who was assimilated to the Pope of Rome, a common accusation at the time.[69]

But in speaking for the Protestants, Émile Petitot called himself a Jewish Christian, a converted Jew, and even an oracle—descriptions that closely matched what he thought of himself during his attacks of mania. He thus became a prophet of the end of the world and set his sights on finding and destroying the Antichrist. However, if it was not true that the Antichrist would appear among the Dené, then possibly the Protestants were right and he should be sought among the Roman Catholics. With this, the framework of the missionary's delirious episodes was in place. Since the conversion of the last hold-outs in the Jewish diaspora had begun, the end of the world was imminent, and to ensure the salvation of humanity, it was necessary to kill the Antichrist. Either he was Jean Séguin, his Oblate colleague, or—cruel irony—Émile Petitot himself.

Thus, the missionary, during his manic periods, begged to be sacrificed. "Nobody managed to sleep," wrote Jean Séguin in 1874 about one of these episodes. "He would not stop calling for someone to smash his head."[70] Three years later, he added:

> During his fits, he keeps on pleading with us to kill him. "Is there no axe or gun," he kept shouting, "to cut off my head or blow it up? After that, everything will be fine!"[71]

Usually, however, Émile Petitot remained more undecided. "He was a crazed madman for six days," Jean Séguin wrote in a letter of January 1871. "Several times he tried to surprise me and grab my neck to strangle me, since one of us had to die to save the world. One of us was the Antichrist, but he didn't know which one."[72] In another letter, Jean Séguin wrote:

> Around midnight, he had an inspiration: one of us had to die to save the human race. He stood up and came over to me, saying that we had to fight until he succumbed. I grasped his body and went to throw him on his bed. He then began to shout loudly enough to be heard from the fort, crying out for help, that he was being murdered. The fit lasted around two hours.
>
> Barely an hour after that, he was seized by another fit of frenzy and he came back to me, saying we had to get it over with quickly, since the end of the world was near. I carried him to his bed again despite the kicks and punches he gave me. I held him down for about an hour, but he struggled so much to pull himself out of my hands that I soon reached the end of my strength. I sent for people from the fort, and thank goodness I did, because if I had still been alone, I probably would have lost him.
>
> On the third night, he threw himself at us at every moment, trying to grab us by the throat, because, he said, there had to be a victim. I gave him a good round of lashes with a whip, after which he quieted down a bit. From time to time, he would advance again, but the idea

of what he had just received made him back down, all the while making threats.

After the men left, I saw him heading for the kitchen. I called out to him and he came back saying that an angel had held his hand. He then began accusing me of having killed our Lord and his mother that same morning and having thrown them into hell. "Justice must be done!" he said as he ran to the kitchen, armed himself with an axe, and came back to the room. When he appeared at the door, I told him I was going to take out the whip again. He looked at me for a moment, during which time I made a move to go get the whip. He then threw down the axe and went back to his room, grinding his teeth.[73]

Unfortunately, Jean Séguin was not always precise in describing his colleague's ideas. It is true that he did not wish to expand too much in his correspondence ("Instead of entrusting to paper the rest of what I have to say, I would much rather tell you in person"), perhaps because he feared that Émile Petitot would open his letters or because they concerned matters that should not be written down.[74] The few letters that did mention them and have come down to us were always accompanied by the words "secret" or "private," and those who wrote them often asked that the letter be burned after reading it. Nevertheless, in another letter, written at the request of his superiors, Jean Séguin returned to this episode and completed his description of what happened:

While I was saying Holy Mass, he went back to the fort to ask one of the enlisted men to come and tie me up, since I was the beast of the apocalypse and I prevented people from going to heaven. Throughout the day, he fixated on the idea of the end of the world, but I cannot tell you everything he argued on this subject. But we were always set in opposition to each other: when I was the beast, he was Jesus Christ or the angel who had to tie it up and throw it into the fire. When I was the angel, he was the beast. Night came but without any sleep. Around midnight, he got up like a madman and came to throw himself upon me, saying he was Jacob and I was the angel and that we were going to fight all night long. I ended up grabbing him and carrying him to his bed. He spent the next day crying, laughing, and doing a thousand crazy things. In the evening, I sent him to bed again, but around eleven o'clock, he got up, like the night before, in a frenzy, screaming in ways that would make you paralyzed with fright, and came to throw himself upon me again. To satisfy God's justice, he said, a victim was needed, and it had to be one of us. He tried to grab me by the neck but missed me.[75]

The next day, the crisis resumed, and the priest continued his quest for "a victim to save the world":

Around six o'clock in the evening, he picked up from the night before: we were at the final stage of the end of the world. He said he no longer doubted I was the Antichrist. I had to be killed, and he was the angel who had to carry out the task.[76]

When Jean Séguin told him to go rest up, the angry priest replied:

"Rest up, how? After having seen you kill Jesus Christ and his mother and cast them into hell, no! No, I'm here to avenge them!" With that, he opened the door, returned to the kitchen, and came back with an axe in his hands.[77]

Despite Émile Petitot's indecision, he usually saw Jean Séguin as the Antichrist, the beast of the apocalypse who kept Christ and his mother in hell and thus obstructed the redemption of humanity. He had to confront this beast by any means necessary. But if Émile Petitot was not the Antichrist, who was he? The Patriarch Jacob who fought with an angel until dawn? The angel who would bring down the beast? The oracle who had received the vision of the conversion of the last Jews, those of the North Pole? The Christ Messiah who asked to be sacrificed and who, by being circumcised, had become both Jewish and Indigenous, an Arctic Jew? At the peak of the missionary's schizoid episodes, it was no longer a matter of ambivalence: identities proliferated, collided, and overlapped in unbridled, hallucinated confusion. After the most violent crises, Jean Séguin, spurred by indescribable repugnance, calmly but systematically summed up the mutations his fallen colleague went through: "For eight days, he thought he was Jewish, Mohammedan, pagan, savage, the Antichrist, Christ, an angel, etc., etc."[78] "During the night, he sometimes became Protestant, sometimes Jewish, sometimes Mohammedan, Buddhist, etc., etc., etc. . . . He then thought he was a wandering Jew."[79] "He was sometimes Jewish, Turkish, Buddhist, the demon, the Antichrist, or the good Lord."[80]

One conviction remained constant in the missionary's prophetic delirium, despite the hyperborean turmoil of evanescent identities: it was essential to save humanity and to do so, he had to hasten the end of the world and precipitate the apocalypse. Émile Petitot never accomplished his plan; it was his own world that collapsed.

★

What is delirium? According to some, it is a mechanical dysfunction in a brain module; according to others, it is a profound alteration of the psyche, which begins to produce false interpretations and perceptions without an object; a temporary swerve off course, obliterating reality in favor of a feared or cherished illusion; a state of extreme exaltation that shatters the levees of consciousness and self, compensating for a primordial frustration and exposing the most buried and secret desires; the solipsistic experience of a reality clothed in an aura of concreteness and disturbing, mute familiarity; a heterogeneous collection of symptoms, impossible to clearly circumscribe but in which an observer, with glasses polished by an era and a milieu, may discern a family resemblance among certain incorrigible ideas and extravagant acts; a stigmatized condition that, under the semblance of a moral order, disguises the iniquities constituting all societies and institutions, thereby legitimizing the confinement and exclusion of marginalized and defiant individuals; or an intolerable suffering sublimated by a thought pattern that continually digresses and subverts the impasses posed by the absence of a creative oeuvre with which to share a self-contained world, bearing witness to a sensitivity and intelligence that goes unrecognized.

Émile Petitot, a voluntary exile, spent his years below the Arctic Circle playing off one delusion against another, simultaneously mitigating and nourishing his acute suffering. He fought off persecutory delusions by developing a delusional theory, one that plunged him into a new form of delirium, this time schizoid, messianic, and frenzied. Inadmissable desires, which ineluctably drove him to chase Dené youths, above all to follow the beautiful Hyacinthe everywhere, clashed head-on with his vows of celibacy, an absurd condition he found unbearable. It emerged from the path he had embraced to become a great nomad freed from all constraints, to go in search of the most distant tribes that were as different as possible from the environment in which he had grown up. He sought to escape the ecclesiastical hierarchy, the sedentary nature of the missions, and the ubiquity of a moral order in which he himself participated and which made him detest his sexual deviance and repeated flights into the wilderness. He was persecuted and he persecuted himself; he had to confess, repent, condemn his actions and thoughts, promise to uphold his status as a White, sedentary, celibate bachelor and contritely keep to the place to which he had been assigned. But he did not succeed: the more he hated himself, the more he saw himself becoming Other and the more he succumbed to the attractions of nomadic life and lovers among the Native inhabitants of the forests surrounding Fort Good Hope.

It is difficult to fix the date when his persecutory delusions began, the moment when the slightest utterance became masked slander or when the supposedly slanderous statements became obscure murder plans. Once this pattern took hold, the missionary was never free of it; the pattern redefined the landmarks of his mental universe, sowed dangers everywhere and populated his inner landscape with nothing but hidden enemies, thus isolating him more and more. Émile Petitot's persecutory delusions should be understood as an interminable protest against priestly celibacy and the rigid morality of postrevolutionary Catholicism, but this did not make it more engaging; his madness was sad and sterile. And if Émile Petitot caught my attention, it is because his delusions proliferated until they far exceeded the simple litany of his more or less imaginary persecutions, attaining an intriguing and extraordinary inventiveness.

To curb the persecutions, to convince his accusers of his innocence and good will, to make himself indispensable by pursuing an objective that he thought he alone could achieve, one with a strategic utility that no one would dispute, Émile Petitot committed himself body and soul to the intellectual study of what he loved. As much fascinated as repelled by the Native mores he encountered, he created an enthusiastic amalgam of personal observations, ethnographic in nature, and risky, self-taught incursions into theological speculation, as candid as they were flawed. The result was a new version of the theory of the Jewish origin of Indigenous peoples of the Americas, a theory once taken seriously and widely discussed but which became, in the nineteenth century, the sole purview of prophets and lunatics.

If Émile Petitot experienced persecution as a painful necessity, he chose the means and method of his salvation on his own. He did not revolt against the social and religious order in the manner of an Indigenous prophet or Louis

Riel, but neither did he join the obedient, condescending, and despotic flock of his Catholic colleagues. Rather, he dedicated himself to composing an immense oeuvre, freezing for eternity, in the silence of Western libraries, the richness and singularity of Dené knowledge and speech, hoping to reveal the existence of the North Pole Jews to a jaded century. This was a new delusion, according to the academic criteria of the day, which relegated him to the great morass of literary madmen. Yet it was a positive, creative delusion, sustained by love and desire for the Other—with "whether Israelite or Indigenous, or both Israelite and Indigenous— and not by fear and suspicion.

Nevertheless, the remedy was also poisonous, since the conversion of the Arctic Jews, the last Hebrew tribes in the diaspora, signaled to the missionary, now an oracle, that the apocalypse was imminent. And so during his episodes of mania, usually occurring in the winter darkness and cold, Émile Petitot, filling up page after page, identified himself more and more with the object of his desire: rather than converting those he believed were Jewish Indians, he converted himself into an Indian Jew. In his final schizoid delirium, violence was no longer simply latent. It exploded against himself, as when he ripped off his clothes in the snow to abolish his identity as a priest, when he mutilated himself or asked to be circumcised, like the Jews of the North Pole, and when he asked to be sacrificed for his own salvation and that of humanity, seeing himself as the Messiah of the end times. It exploded against others, against his missionary alter ego in particular, the dull and homely Jean Séguin, whom he saw as the Antichrist, the beast of the apocalypse, the ultimate enemy whose defeat would inaugurate a new millennial reign, a world without suffering or delirium, something Émile Petitot desired more than anything.

The end of the world took place in the form of an internment in an insane asylum. Émile Petitot, now a failed prophet, could no longer see the Dené and no longer fantasize about being a Jew wandering in the tundra snow.

His exile was internal; having been persecuted, reduced to silence and solitude, he cherished his last outlet, the writing of his most ambitious and deranged work, which he considered the most momentous of his times. In this work, he wove together one last time all the links he had discovered and laid out in his memoirs, all the proofs he had found in the Bible and elsewhere, all the analogies he had perceived in the chaos of his wild and jumbled scholarship, assembling a concordance of the myths in the cosmogony of the Arctic Danites, whom he would have liked to simply call the Arctic Jews.

★

On Émile Petitot's gravestone, located in Mareuil-lès-Meaux, Seine-et-Marne, a cast iron plaque with rusty bolts reminds us that the parish priest of Haute-Brie was also an "Arctic missionary and explorer." As I read these words, I wonder what I came to do in this cramped cemetery and, at the same time, why I wrote this book. Early on, I was impressed by the bilingual collections of Indigenous myths that the priest published, sensing I had discovered a predecessor, even a precursor, where I did not expect it at all. Not wanting to write a life story, I found that, by retracing the biography of a delirium, I could revive an old fascination for antipsychiatry, a liberating approach that considers the words and acts of madness as committed expressions by a singular voice that needs to be heard—which is why it was necessary to include a great many quotations—rather than as bundles of symptoms to organize hierarchically into a clinical profile. This reasoned flirtation with knowledge gone mad once again provided me, after writing *Lettres mortes*, with the opportunity to question the limits, this time historical, epistemological, and psychiatric, of scientific knowledge and its authorized institutions.[81] Yet I do not stand before this tomb to meditate; I have come to measure the breadth of a disaster.

It was in a village of five hundred souls that Émile Petitot's dreams and illusions ran aground. Released from the mental institution near Montreal in the spring of 1883, he was repatriated to France where, in the capital, he tried to live by his pen, hiding his gnawing feelings of repulsion and horror toward the clergy in general and bishops in particular. His failure came quickly, and so, disenchanted, he resigned himself to spending the last thirty years of his life in entrenched solitude, as far from the Dené as from his family, a heartless old polar bear reciting Mass every morning at seven o'clock, writing up his memoirs at nightfall, and cultivating a bitter nostalgia for "his savages" over the years.[82] The contrast is striking between his twenty years of wanderings in the boreal region, rich in amorous passions and new ideas, and his last thirty years of immobility and slow fossilization, which soon led to silence and paralysis—the disparity between the hallucinated fertility of the Arctic snows and the narrow-minded sterility of the Briard countryside. Émile Petitot, who knew nothing but feverish dissatisfaction his whole life, exhausted himself in a madness that gradually dissipated behind the altar of the church in Mareuil, under the dismayed but compassionate gaze of a figure of Saint Sebastian, with his unsettling tilted hips, his naked torso pierced by an arrow—the final doleful echo of the exiled lover, his fantasized martyrdom, and his tragic madness.

Notes

Notes to Chapter One

1. Émile Petitot to the Marquise de Vatimesnil, written from Longue Pointe Asylum near Montreal, dated March 31, 1882 (Richelieu, Canada: Archives Deschâtelets-Notre-Dame-du-Cap, hereinafter "Archives Deschâlets").

2. Émile Petitot, *En route pour la mer glaciale* (Paris: Letouzey & Ané, 1888), 91.

3. Petitot, *En route*, 91.

4. Petitot, *En route*, 91–92.

5. Petitot, *En route*, 92–93.

6. Petitot, *En route*, 93–95.

7. Petitot's missionary colleague Jean Séguin mentioned these *Mémoires d'un missionnaire* early on, in a letter to Faraud, February 5, 1874, from Our Lady of Good Hope Mission (Archives Deschâtelets).

8. Concerning the school on Rue Saint-Savournin, see Régis Bertrand, "Émile Petitot (1838–1916) avant ses missions canadiennes: Origine et formation d'un missionnaire oblat," in *La mission et le sauvage: Huguenots et catholiques d'une rive atlantique à l'autre, xvie–xixe*, ed. Nicole Lemaître (Paris, Québec: CTHS, Presses de l'Université de Laval, 2008), p. 295; see also Régis Bertrand, "Quelques notes sur les origines, la famille et l'enfance d'Émile Petitot" (Rome: General Archives of the Oblates of Mary Immaculate, hereafter OMI General Archives).

9. For information about Émile Petitot's life, see section III in Bibliography, "Biographical Works about Émile Petitot."

10. Although the colonists' labels reified group identities and are imperfectly correlated with current ethnonyms, the First Nations people related to the historical Peaux-de-Lievre or Hareskins nowadays use the self-designation K'asho Got'ine, while various First Nations tracing their ties to the former Loucheux or Kutchin prefer to call themselves Gwich'in ("inhabitant") of a particular location (e.g., Nihtat Gwich'in, Dendu Gwich'in) and to refer to themselves collectively as Dinjii Zhuh.

11. Petitot, *En route*, 236–37.

12. Émile Petitot, *Autour du Grand lac des Esclaves* (Paris: A. Savine, 1891), 230.

13. Petitot, *Autour du Grand lac*, 208.

14. Petitot, *Autour du Grand lac*, 231.

15. Petitot, *Autour du Grand lac*, 231–32.

16. Petitot to Faraud, Lac Klérit'ie, from a spot eleven days west of Fort Rae, June 1, 1864 (Archives Deschâtelets); see also Petitot's letter to De Semallé, Paris, March 13, 1884 (OMI General Archives).

17. Petitot to Faraud, Lac Klérit'ie, from a spot eleven days west of Fort Rae, June 1, 1864 (Archives Deschâtelets); see also Petitot's letter to de Semallé, Paris, March 13, 1884 (OMI General Archives).

18. Émile Petitot, *Exploration de la région du Grand lac des Ours* (Paris: Téqui, 1893), 319–20.

19. Petitot, *Exploration*, 319–20.

20. Clut to Fabre (quoting Petitot's words), St. Michael's Mission, Fort Rae, May 20, 1872 (Archives Deschâtelets); Petitot, *Autour du Grand lac*, 126.

21. Petitot, *Quinze ans*, 167.

22. Petitot to Faraud, Fort Good Hope, September 7, 1864 (Archives Deschâtelets).

23. Faraud to Fabre, Providence Mission, November 15, 1865; Séguin to Faraud, Our Lady of Good Hope Mission, February 18, 1870; Séguin to Faraud, Our Lady of Good Hope Mission, June 3, 1870; Séguin to Faraud, Our Lady of Good Hope Mission, July 25, 1870; Séguin to Faraud, Our Lady of Good Hope Mission, July 27, 1872; Clut to Sardou, Fort Yukon, April 1, 1873 (all letters cited here are located in the Archives Deschâtelets).

24. Petitot, *Quinze ans*, 125–30.

25. Faraud to Fabre, Providence Mission, November 29, 1868 (Archives Deschâtelets).

26. Petitot to Faraud, Fort Good Hope, January 15, 1866 (Archives Deschâtelets).

27. Petitot to Fabre, Our Lady of Good Hope Mission, September 12, 1866 (OMI General Archives).

28. Petitot to Faraud, Fort Good Hope, February 28, 1867 (OMI General Archives).

29. Clut to Faraud, Fort Good Hope, January 2, 1872; Lecorre to Clut, Fort Good Hope, July 29, 1872; Faraud to Fabre, Providence Mission, November 29, 1868 (all located in the Archives Deschâtelets).

30. Petitot to Faraud, Our Lady of Good Hope Mission, January 31, 1868 (Archives Deschâtelets).

31. Hyacinthe Dzanyou, a Hareskin of the Rocky Mountains, to Petitot, dated February 1874, received in Montreal the following July 24, published in *Les missions catholiques* 220 (1874): 635, and reprinted in "Athabaska-Mackenzie," *Les missions catholiques* 329 (1875): 463–65.

32. Petitot to Faraud, Fort Good Hope, January 15, 1866 (Archives Deschâtelets).

33. Émile Petitot, *Accord des mythologies dans la cosmogonie des Danites arctiques* (Paris: E. Bouillon, 1890), 364.

34. Petitot to Faraud, Fort Good Hope, January 15, 1866 (Archives Deschâtelets).

35. Petitot to Fabre, Our Lady of Good Hope Mission, July 12, 1866 (OMI General Archives); Faraud to Fabre, Slave River, July 8, 1866 (Archives Deschâtelets); Séguin to Faraud, Our Lady of Good Hope Mission, August 2, 1866 (Archives Deschâtelets); Clut to Faraud, Providence Mission, November 14, 1873 (Archives Deschâtelets).

36. Petitot to Faraud, Fort Good Hope, January 15, 1866; Petitot to Faraud, Our Lady of Good Hope Mission, January 31, 1868; Petitot to Faraud, Île-à-la-Crosse, August 14, 1873; Petitot to Faraud, Providence Mission, January 14, 1879 (all located in the Archives Deschâtelets).

37. Petitot to Faraud, May 1868, Saint Theresa's Mission, Great Bear Lake (Archives Deschâtelets).

38. Émile Petitot, *Les grands Esquimaux* (Paris: Plon, 1887), translated into English by E. O. Hahn as *Among the Chiglit Eskimos*, 2nd ed. (Edmonton: University of Alberta Press, Boreal Institute, 1999). For a detailed review of the book, see Victor Philippe's letter to Gaston Carrière, Fort Smith, August 20, 1983, to which is apprended an unpublished study, "Le Père Émile Petitot et les Esquimaux" (Richelieu, Canada: Archives Deschâtelets-Notre-Dame-Du-Cap).

39. Petitot, *Les grands Esquimaux*, 40–41.

40. Petitot, *Accord des mythologies*, 354.

41. Petitot, *Accord des mythologies*, 354.

42. Petitot, *Les grands Esquimaux*, 90–91.

43. Petitot to Faraud, Saint Theresa's Mission, Great Bear Lake, May 30, 1868 (Archives Deschâtelets).

44. Adrien-Gabriel Morice, *Histoire de l'Église catholique dans l'Ouest canadien, du Lac Supérieur au Pacifique (1659–1905)*, vol. 2 (Winnipeg: Chez l'auteur, 1912), 540.

45. Petitot to Faraud, Saint Theresa's Mission, May 30, 1868. See also Séguin's letter to Faraud, Our Lady of Good Hope Mission, September 16, 1869; Faraud to Fabre, Providence Mission, November 27, 1869; Clut to Faraud, Nativity Mission, February 15, 1869; Séguin

to Faraud, Our Lady of Good Hope Mission, February 18, 1870; Petitot to Faraud, Our Lady of Good Hope Mission, February 28, 1870; Clut to Fabre, Montreal, April 29, 1870; Clut to Faraud, Nativity Mission, March 21, 1871; Séguin to Faraud, Our Lady of Good Hope Mission, June 3, 1870; Séguin to Fabre, Our Lady of Good Hope Mission, May 25, 1871 (OMI General Archives); Kearney to Faraud, Our Lady of Good Hope Mission, June 3, 1872; Clut to Faraud, Fort Good Hope, September 11, 1871; Petitot to Faraud, Fort Good Hope, January 8, 1877; Séguin to Faraud, Our Lady of Good Hope Mission, May 25, 1875; Séguin to Faraud, Our Lady of Good Hope Mission, February 1, 1877; Petitot to Faraud, Providence Mission, January 14, 1879; Séguin to Fabre, Fort Good Hope, February 5, 1879 (OMI General Archives); Séguin to Clut, on the small lake near Providence Mission, September 23, 1879 (OMI General Archives) (unless otherwise noted, all letters cited here are located in the Archives Deschâtelets).

46. Petitot, *En route*, 5; Petitot, *Autour du Grand lac*, 208.

47. Petitot to Fabre, Fort Good Hope, September 15, 1869, *Missions de la Congrégation des Missionnaires Oblats de Marie Immaculée* 35 (1870): 296–98.

48. Séguin to Faraud, Our Lady of Good Hope Mission, September 16, 1869 (Archives Deschâtelets).

49. Séguin to Faraud, Our Lady of Good Hope Mission, June 3, 1870 (Archives Deschâtelets).

50. Kearney to Faraud, Our Lady of Good Hope Mission, June 3, 1872 (Archives Deschâtelets).

51. Clut to Fabre, Saint Michael's Mission, Fort Rae, May 20, 1872 (Archives Deschâtelets).

52. Séguin to Faraud, Our Lady of Good Hope Mission, July 25, 1870 (Archives Deschâtelets).

53. Robert Choquette, *The Oblate Assault on Canada's Northwest* (Ottawa: University of Ottawa Press, 1995), 65.

54. Petitot to Faraud, Fort Good Hope, January 8, 1877 (Archives Deschâtelets).

55. The works Petitot wrote at the time were, in particular, *Les grands Esquimaux* and *Quinze ans sous le cercle polaire*.

56. Panaccio to Savoie, Montreal, March 6, 1973 (Archives Deschâtelets).

57. About François-Xavier Perrault, see André Paradis, "L'asile de 1845 à 1920," in *L'institution médicale,* ed. Normand Séguin (Quebec: Presses de l'Université de Laval, 1998), 50–57.

58. Petitot to his sister Fortunée, Longue Pointe Asylum, February 25, 1882 (Archives Deschâtelets).

59. About Dr. Howard, see Rodrigue Samuel, "Henry Howard," in *Dictionnaire biographique du Canada*, vol. 11 (Quebec, Toronto: Presses de l'Université Laval, University of Toronto, 1982); André Paradis, "L'asile de 1845 à 1920," 50–57.

60. Petitot to his sister Fortunée, Longue Pointe Asylum, near Montreal, February 25, 1882 (Archives Deschâtelets).

61. Petitot to his sister Fortunée, Longue Pointe Asylum, February 25, 1882; see also Petitot's letter to the Consul at the French Consulate in Montreal, Longue Pointe Asylum, March 1, 1882; Petitot to his brother Auguste, Longue Pointe Asylum, March 3, 1882; Petitot to Taché, Longue Pointe Asylum, March 10, 1882 (all letters located in the Archives Deschâtelets).

62. Daniel Hack Tuke, *The Insane in the United States and Canada* (London: H. K. Lewis, 1893), 195.

63. Tuke, *The Insane*, 189–201; see also Daniel Francis, "A Victorian Scandal: The Asylum at Longue Pointe," *The Beaver* 69, no. 3 (1989): 33–38; André Paradis, "L'asile de 1845 à 1920," 37–74.

64. Joseph-Charles Taché, *Les asiles d'aliénés de la province de Québec et leurs détracteurs* (Quebec: Hull, 1885), 30.

65. Petitot to his sister Fortunée, Longue Pointe Asylum, February 25, 1882 (Archives Deschâtelets).

66. Petitot to a cousin (probably Émile Dardy), Longue Pointe Asylum, March 31, 1882 (Archives Deschâtelets).

Notes to Chapter Two

1. Petitot, *En route*, 12.

2. Petitot, *En route*, 12–13.

3. Petitot, *En route*, 13–14.

4. Petitot, September 1863, *Missions de la Congrégation des Missionnaires Oblats de Marie Immaculée* 23 (1867): 370–71.

5. Claude Champagne, *Les débuts de la mission dans le Nord-Ouest canadien: Mission et Église chez Mgr Vital Grandin, o.m.i., 1829–1902* (Ottawa: Éditions de l'Université Saint-Paul, 1983), 83.

6. Émile Grouard, *Souvenirs de mes soixante ans d'Apostolat dans l'Athabaska-Mackenzie* (Lyon: Œuvres Apostoliques, 1923), 143.

7. Pierre-Jean De Smet, *Notice sur le territoire et sur la mission de l'Orégon* (Bruxelles: Bureau de Publication de la Bibliothèque d'Éducation, 1847), 171–80; see also Denis Gagnon and Lynn Drapeau, "Les échelles catholiques comme exemples de métissage religieux des ontologies chrétiennes et amérindiennes," *Studies in Religion* 44, no. 2 (2015): 178–207.

8. Émile Petitot, *Traditions indiennes du Canada Nord-Ouest: Textes originaux et traductions littérales* (Alençon: E. Renaut de Broise, 1887), 93, 98.

9. Émile Petitot, *Traditions indiennes du Canada Nord-Ouest* (Paris: Maisonneuve, 1886), 112, 108.

10. Luc Boltanski, Énigmes et complots (Paris: Gallimard, 2012).

11. Émile Petitot, "Étude sur la nation montagnaise," *Missions de la Congrégation des Missionnaires Oblats de Marie Immaculée* 24 (1867): 490–91.

12. Émile Grouard, *Souvenirs de mes soixante ans d'Apostolat*, 143.

13. Petitot, *Autour du Grand lac*, 98.

14. Émile Petitot, "Les Esquimaux," *Compte rendu du Congrès international des Américanistes*, vol. 1 (Nancy: Gustave Crépin-Leblond, 1875), 330.

15. Émile Grouard, "Le R. P. Petitot et le R. P. Grouard au Congrès de Nancy," *Missions de la Congrégation des Missionnaires Oblats de Marie Immaculée* 51 (1875): 397–419.

16. Petitot, *Exploration*, 150; Petitot to Rey, Fort Good Hope, May 10, 1870, *Missions de la Congrégation des Missionnaires Oblats de Marie Immaculée* 36 (1871): 372–75; Émile Petitot, "Les Déné-Dindjiés," *Compte-rendu du Congrès international des Américanistes*, vol. 2 (Nancy: Gustave Crépin-Leblond, 1875), 26–37.

17. Petitot, *Traditions . . . Textes* (1887), 266–67.

18. Petitot, *Traditions* (1886), 274–75.

19. Petitot, "Étude sur la nation montagnaise," 505–6, 508.

20. Editor, *Revue critique d'histoire et de littérature: Recueil hebdomadaire* 31, no. 13 (March 30, 1891): n.p.

21. Petitot, *Autour du Grand lac*, 110–11.

22. Émile Petitot, "Souvenirs de Provence," unpublished manuscript (Richelieu, Canada: Archives Deschâtelets-Notre-Dame-du-Cap, 1856).

23. Petitot to Rey, Fort Good Hope, 10 May 1870, *Missions de la Congrégation des Missionnaires Oblats de Marie Immaculée* 36 (1871): 372–75.

24. Petitot, "Les Déné-Dindjiés," 16; Petitot to Rey, Fort Good Hope, May 10, 1870, *Missions de la Congrégation des Missionnaires Oblats de Marie Immaculée* 36 (1871): 375.

25. Petitot, "Du même auteur, en préparation," *En route*, n.p.

26. Petitot, *Autour du Grand lac*, 306–7.

27. Petitot, *Traditions . . . Textes* (1887), 307–8.

28. Petitot, *Traditions* (1886), 317–18.

29. Petitot, Our Lady of Good Hope Mission, February 29, 1868, *Missions de la Congrégation des Missionnaires Oblats de Marie Immaculée* 31 (1869): 310. See also Séguin to Faraud, Our Lady of Good Hope Mission, July 25, 1870; Petitot, Our Lady of Good Hope Mission, July 30, 1869, *Missions de la Congrégation des Missionnaires Oblats de Marie Immaculée* 34 (1870): 208–9; Kearney to Faraud, Mission of Our Lady of Good Hope Mission, September 8, 1870; Séguin to Clut, Fort Good Hope, January 24, 1871, cited in letter from Clut to Fabre, Nativity Mission, May 14, 1871; Eynard to Faraud, Providence Mission, 24 March 1872; Séguin to Faraud, Our Lady of Good Hope Mission, July 2, 1877 (unless otherwise noted, all letters cited here are located in the Archives Deschâtelets).

30. Séguin to Faraud, Our Lady of Good Hope Mission, July 25, 1870 (Archives Deschâtelets).

31. Séguin to Faraud, Our Lady of Good Hope Mission, February 9, 1877 (Archives Deschâtelets); see also Séguin to Fabre, Our Lady of Good Hope Mission, May 25, 1871 (OMI General Archives).

32. Petitot to Faraud, Our Lady of Good Hope Mission, January 31, 1868 (Archives Deschâtelets).

33. Séguin to Faraud, Our Lady of Good Hope Mission, July 27, 1872 (Archives Deschâtelets).

34. Séguin to Faraud, Our Lady of Good Hope Mission, July 27, 1872 (Archives Deschâtelets).

35. Petitot, *Traditions . . . Textes* (1887), 309–10.

36. Petitot, *Traditions* (1886), 319–20.

37. Clut to Faraud, Fort Good Hope, January 2, 1872 (Archives Deschâtelets).

38. Clut to Fabre, St. Michael's Mission, Fort Rae, May 20, 1872 (Archives Deschâtelets).

39. Clut to Fabre, St. Michael's Mission, Fort Rae, May 20, 1872 (Archives Deschâtelets).

40. Clut to Faraud, Fort Yukon, August 1, 1873, copied from letter from Clut to Sardou, April 1 (Archives Deschâtelets); see also Clut to Faraud, Providence Mission, November 14, 1873 (Archives Deschâtelets).

41. Petitot, *Traditions . . . Textes* (1887), 324–25.

42. Petitot, *Traditions* (1886), 332–33, where Émile Petitot added: "This legend obviously brings together the ancient and universal memory of the confusion of languages with the memory of a more recent event, a terrible volcanic eruption, followed by a collapse that would have taken place not far from the Pacific Ocean, in the western part of the great continental cordillera of America."

43. Petitot to his sister Fortunée, Longue Pointe Asylum, February 25, 1882 (Archives Deschâtelets).

44. Émile Petitot, *Origine et migrations des peuples de la Gaule jusqu'à l'avènement des Francs* (Paris: J. Maisonneuve, 1894), iv; Savoie to Olivier, Ottawa, October 20, 1976 (Archives Deschâtelets).

45. Gustave Aymard was the author of many popular novels, among them, *Les trappeurs de l'Arkansas* (1858), *Le fils du soleil* (1879), and *Les bandits de l'Arizona* (1881). He died while interned at Saint Anne's Hospital in 1883.

46. Petitot, *Exploration*, v.

47. Régis Bertrand, "Émile Petitot: Le retour définitif en France (1883–1886) et la cure de Mareuil-lès-Meaux (1886–1916)," *Revue d'Histoire et d'Art de la Brie et du Pays de Meaux* 26 (1975): 67.

48. Editors, "Missions du Mackenzie," *Missions de la Congrégation des Missionnaires Oblats de Marie Immaculée* 35 (1870): 270.

49. Émile Grouard, "Le R. P. Petitot et le R. P. Grouard au Congrès de Nancy."

50. Émile Petitot, "Six légendes américaines identifiées à l'histoire de Moïse et du peuple hébreu," *Missions de la Congrégation des Missionnaires Oblats de Marie Immaculée* 60, supplement (1877): 586.

51. Petitot, "Six légendes américaines," 692.

52. Émile Petitot, "Sur l'habitat et les fluctuations de la population peau rouge, en Canada," *Bulletin et mémoires de la Société d'anthropologie de Paris* 7 (1884): 223 (discussion).

53. Gabriel Gravier, *L'abbé Petitot chez les grands Esquimaux* (Rouen: Espérance Cagnard, 1888), 34–35.

54. Henry Carnoy, review of *Accord des mythologies dans la cosmogonie des Danites arctiques*, by Émile Petitot, *La tradition* 5 (1891): 95.

55. Albert Réville, review of *Accord des mythologies dans la cosmogonie des Danites arctiques*, by Émile Petitot, *Revue de l'histoire des religions* 22 (1890): 223–24.

56. Petitot to Fabre, Our Lady of Good Hope Mission, September 12, 1866 (OMI General Archives).

57. Émile Petitot, *Dictionnaire de la langue dènè-dindjié* (Paris: E. Leroux, 1876).

58. Petitot, *Traditions . . . Textes* (1887), passim; see also Petitot, *Autour du Grand lac*, 108.

59. These were his *Traditions indiennes du Canada Nord-Ouest: Textes originaux et traductions littérales* (1887) and *Traditions indiennes du Canada Nord-Ouest* (1886), respectively.

60. Petitot, *Accord des mythologies*, 20; Petitot, *Traditions* (1886), vii.

61. Ralph Maud, *A Guide to B. C. Indian Myth and Legend* (Vancouver: Talonbooks, 1982).

Notes to Chapter Three

1. Menasseh ben Israel, *The Hope of Israel*, ed. Henry Méchoulan and Gérard Nahon, trans. Moses Wall (Oxford: Oxford University Press, [1650] 1987), 109.

2. Ben Israel, *Hope of Israel*, 113.

3. Ben Israel, *Hope of Israel*, 121, 176–77.

4. Ben Israel, *Hope of Israel*, 160, 164, 172–73.

5. Henry Méchoulan and Gérard Nahon, "Introduction," ben Israel, *Hope of Israel*, 46–47.

6. Méchoulan and Nahon, "Introduction," ben Israel, Hope of Israel, 44, 48–49.

7. Méchoulan and Nahon, "Introduction," ben Israel, *Hope of Israel*, 56–57, 64, 90.

8. Richard H. Popkin, "The Rise and Fall of the Jewish Indian Theory," in *Menasseh ben Israel and his World*, ed. Yosef Kaplan, Henry Méchoulan, and Richard H. Popkin (Leiden: Brill, 1989), 63–82; see also Richard H. Popkin, "Jewish Messianism and Christian Millenarianism," in *Culture and Politics from Puritanism to the Enlightenment*, ed. Perez Zagorin (Berkeley: University of California Press, 1980), 67–90. On the lost tribes of Israel, see Allen H. Godbey, *The Lost Tribes, A Myth: Suggestions towards Rewriting Hebrew History* (Durham, NC: Duke University Press, 1930). On the "theory of the Jewish Indians," see Robert Wauchope, *Lost Tribes and Sunken Continents: Myth and Method in the Study of American Indians* (Chicago: University of Chicago Press, 1962); Lee Eldridge Huddleston, *Origins of the American Indians: European Concepts, 1492–1729* (Austin: University of Texas Press, 1967).

9. Émile Petitot, "Étude sur la nation montagnaise," 516–20; on Abbot Migne's publications, see R. Howard Bloch, *Le plagiaire de Dieu* (Paris: Seuil, 1996).

10. Petitot to Rey, Providence Mission (Mackenzie River rapids), August 18, 1869, *Missions de la Congrégation des*

Missionnaires Oblats de Marie Immaculée 35 (1870): 294. In *Traditions* (1886), xvii, Émile Petitot speaks of the survival of the blood of Abraham among the Dené in these terms: "The blood of Israel, a providential buoy for the troubled, the downtrodden, the shipwrecked of the faith; a seed thrown into the desert to bear fruit alone and to be reaped in its own time, according to the word of Jahowah, faithful to Jacob and David: *Si ad cardines coeli* (the Foot of the Sky, the poles) *dissipatus fueris, inde te retraham, dicit Dominus exercituum* (Deuteronomy 28:61)." Note that it is actually from Deuteronomy 30:4.

11. Petitot, *Quinze ans*, 149.

12. On the messianic movements among the Dené, see John Webster Grant, "Missionaries and Messiahs in the Northwest," *Studies in Religion* 9, no. 2 (1980): 125–36; Kerry Abel, "Prophets, Priests and Preachers: Dene Shamans and Christian Missions in the Nineteenth Century," *Historical Papers* 21, no. 1 (1986): 211–24; June Helm, *Prophecy and Power among the Dogrib Indians* (Lincoln: University of Nebraska Press, 1994), 60–64; Martha McCarthy, *From the Great River to the Ends of the Earth: The Missionary Oblates of Mary Immaculate in the Canadian North West* (Edmonton: University of Alberta Press, 1995).

13. Dom Benoit, *Vie de Mgr Taché*, vol. 1 (Montreal: Librairie Beauchemin, 1904), 399–402.

14. Benoit, *Vie de Mgr Taché*, 399–402; see also Champagne, *Les débuts de la mission dans le Nord-Ouest canadien*, 164–67.

15. Petitot, *En route*, 268–69.

16. Petitot, *En route*, 269.

17. Petitot, May 1864, *Missions de la Congrégation des Missionnaires Oblats de Marie Immaculée* 24 (1867): 461–63; Petitot, *Autour du Grand lac*, 225. See also Petitot to Faraud, Lake Klérit'ie, eleven days west of Fort Rae, June 1, 1864; "Missions d'Amérique," *Annales de la propagation*

de la foi 37 (1865): 383–84; Séguin, Our Lady of Good Hope Mission, May 27, 1872 (Archives Deschâtelets); Séguin to Faraud, Our Lady of Good Hope Mission, February 4, 1874 (Archives Deschâtelets).

18. Petitot, *Autour du Grand lac*, 226. For an account of the prophetic movements of the Dogribs in the 1960s, see June Helm, *Prophecy and Power*, 61–62.

19. Fernand Michel, *Dix huit ans chez les sauvages: Voyages et missions de M. Henry Faraud* (Paris: Régis Ruffet, 1866), 113; see also Scott Rushforth, "The Legitimation of Beliefs in a Hunter-Gatherer Society," *American Ethnologist* 19, no. 3 (1992): 483–500.

20. Extracts from letter from R. P. Petitot to T. R. P. Superior General, *Missions de la Congrégation des Missionnaires Oblats de Marie Immaculée* 65 (1879): 6–7.

21. Petitot, *Autour du Grand lac*, 223–26; see also 118.

22. Petitot, *Quinze ans*, 208–9.

23. Petitot, *Exploration*, 172.

24. Petitot, Our Lady of Good Hope Mission, July 30, 1869, *Missions de la Congrégation des Missionnaires Oblats de Marie Immaculée* 34 (1870): 208–9.

25. Prosper Despine, *De la folie au point de vue philosophique ou plus spécialement psychologique étudiée chez le malade et chez l'homme en santé* (Paris: F. Savy, 1875), 725.

26. Petitot, *Exploration*, 380.

27. Petitot, *Exploration*, 425–26.

28. Émile Petitot, *Monographie des Déné-Dindjiés* (Paris: Ernest Leroux, 1876), 31–32.

29. Émile Saindon, *En missionnant: Essai sur les missions des Pères Oblats de Marie Immaculée à la Baie James* (Ottawa: Imprimerie du Droit, 1928), 28–29.

30. Jean Malaurie, *Les derniers rois de Thulé* (Paris: Plon, 1955), 135.

31. Petitot to Faraud, St. Raphael's Church, April 15, 1881 (OMI General Archives).

32. Séguin to Clut, Fort Good Hope, January 24, 1871, cited in letter from Clut to Fabre, Nativity Mission, May 14, 1871 (Archives Deschâtelets).

33. Séguin to Faraud, Our Lady of Good Hope Mission, July 25, 1870 (Archives Deschâtelets).

34. Séguin to Clut, Fort Good Hope, January 24, 1871, cited in letter from Clut to Fabre, Nativity Mission, May 14, 1871 (Archives Deschâtelets).

35. Eynard to Faraud, Providence Mission, March 24, 1872 (Archives Deschâtelets).

36. Despine, *De la folie au point de vue philosophique*, 719–40.

37. Petitot to Rey, Providence Mission (Mackenzie River rapids), August 18, 1869, *Missions de la Congrégation des Missionnaires Oblats de Marie Immaculée* 35 (1870): 294.

38. Alexander Mackenzie, *Voyages from Montreal, on the River St. Laurence, through the Continent of North America, to the Frozen and Pacific Oceans, in the Years 1789 and 1793*, vol. 1 (London: T. Cadell & W. Davies, 1802), 198.

39. Petitot to Rey, Fort Good Hope, May 10, 1870, *Missions de la Congrégation des Missionnaires Oblats de Marie Immaculée* 36 (1871): 372–75.

40. Émile Petitot, "Les Déné-Dindjiés," 25.

41. Petitot, *Traditions* (1886), 260.

42. "Les petits garçons naissent, alors un peu forts lorsqu'ils sont, leur visage est carminé lorsque, le tremblement contre leur verge-peau on tranchait un silex avec. Puis une alène avec leurs bras aussi, leurs joues aussi on perçait, leurs oreilles aussi, leur nez-cartilage aussi on transperçait." Petitot, *Traditions ... Textes* (1887), 249–50.

43. Petitot, *Traditions ... Textes* (1887), 250.

44. Petitot, *Quinze ans*, 311.

45. Émile Grouard, *Souvenirs de mes soixante ans d'Apostolat*, 144; see also the account by the Oblate missionary Xavier Georges Ducot about the Dené Hareskins: "The savages do not know a thing about what circumcision is," in letter from Ducot to Lestanc, Fort Good Hope, January 1879 (OMI General Archives).

46. Séguin to Faraud, Our Lady of Good Hope Mission, February 5, 1874 (Archives Deschâtelets).

47. Séguin to Fabre, Fort Good Hope, June 3, 1874 (OMI General Archives).

48. Séguin to Faraud, Our Lady of Good Hope Mission, February 9, 1877 (Archives Deschâtelets).

49. Séguin to Clut, Our Lady of Good Hope Mission, September 23, 1878 (OMI General Archives).

50. Séguin to Clut, Our Lady of Good Hope Mission, September 23, 1878 (OMI General Archives).

51. Séguin to Clut, Our Lady of Good Hope Mission, February 6, 1879 (Archives Deschâtelets).

52. Lecorre to Faraud, Providence Mission, December 3, 1878 (Archives Deschâtelets); see also Lecorre to Faraud, Providence Mission, January 17, 1879 (Archives Deschâtelets); Ducot to Lestanc, Fort Good Hope, January 30, 1879 (OMI General Archives); Clut to Fabre, Lyon, March 14, 1879 (OMI General Archives); Gascon to Taché, St. Joseph's Mission, April 2, 1879 (OMI General Archives).

53. Petitot, *Accord des mythologies*, 354.

54. Simon Winchester, *The Professor and the Madman* (New York: Harper Perennial, 1998).

55. Ducot to Faraud, Fort Good Hope, August 19, 1878 (OMI General Archives); Séguin to Faraud, Providence Mission, September 19, 1878 (OMI General Archives); Séguin to Clut, Fort Good Hope, September 23, 1878 (OMI General Archives): "He said to me: 'It's a mystery that I don't quite understand yet, but it seems

to me that it must be like a spiritual marriage; since I have done wrong by the weaker sex, I need to make amends.'" See also Gascon to Clut, St. Joseph's Mission, April 3, 1879 (OMI General Archives); Bourgine to Grandin, St. Francis Régis Mission, n.d. (1881) (OMI General Archives); Faraud to Clut, Our Lady of Victories Mission, December 20, 1881 (Archives Deschâtelets); Faraud to Clut, Our Lady of Victories Mission, November 18, 1882 (Archives Deschâtelets); Petitot to Taché, Longue Pointe Asylum, March 10, 1882 (Archives Deschâtelets); Petitot to the Marquise de Vatimesnil, Longue Pointe Asylum, March 30, 1882 (Archives Deschâtelets); Petitot to Auguste Petitot, Longue Pointe Asylum, July 25, 1882 (OMI General Archives). On this subject, see Murielle Nagy, "Le désir de l'Autre chez le missionnaire Émile Petitot," Éros et tabou: Sexualité et genre chez les Amérindiens et les Inuit, ed. Frédéric Laugrand and Gilles Havard (Quebec: Septentrion, 2014), 408–30.

56. This is perhaps what Émile Petitot himself thought, according to a letter he sent from Marseilles to Vital Grandin at the end of his stay at Longue Pointe Asylum. It contains the only sentence I found where he explicitly mentions his circumcision and seems to connect it to his late rejection of homosexuality. Significantly, it is one of the few incoherent sentences in Émile Petitot's correspondence and, although I can guarantee the accuracy of the transcription, I am still unable to reconstruct its exact meaning with certainty: "Vous saviez que j'étais circoncis et avais pris pour la circoncision que j'abhorrais les pratiques sodomiques que vous et quelques autres de vos collaborateurs soutenaient" [You knew that I was circumcised and was focused on circumcision that I abhorred the sodomy practices that you and some of your other collaborators supported]. Petitot to Grandin, Marseille, January 12, 1884 (OMI General Archives).

57. Ducot to Faraud, Fort Good Hope, August 19, 1878 (OMI General Archives).

58. Séguin to Faraud, Providence Mission, September 19, 1878 (OMI General Archives).

59. Gascon to Clut, St. Joseph's Mission, April 3, 1879 (OMI General Archives).

60. Petitot to the Scholastic brothers and their moderator priest, July 23, 1862, *Missions de la Congrégation des Missionnaires Oblats de Marie Immaculée* 6 (1863): 217.

61. Petitot, *Traditions* (1886), 256

62. See J. A. Chapleau, *Discours de l'Hon. J. A. Chapleau, M. P., sur l'exécution de Louis Riel* (Ottawa: McLean, Roger, 1886), 36; Henry Howard, "Histoire médicale de Louis David Riel," *L'étendard* (July 13, 1886), 1.

63. The following facts about Louis Riel come from Gilles Martel, *Le messianisme de Louis Riel* (Waterloo: Wilfrid Laurier University Press, 1984), unless otherwise noted.

64. Alexandre Taché, *La situation au Nord-Ouest* (Quebec: J. O. Filteau, 1885), 17.

65. Third letter from Bishop Grandin, *Le véritable Riel* (Montreal: Imprimerie générale, 1887), 41–42.

66. David Graham Cooper, *The Language of Madness* (London: Penguin Random House, 1980), 23.

67. Petitot, *Autour du Grand lac*, 98–100.

68. Petitot, *Accord des mythologies*, 456.

69. Journal of Bishop Grandin, on the Liard River, August 26, 1861, *Missions de la Congrégation des Missionnaires Oblats de Marie Immaculée* 9 (1864): 225; Grouard, *Souvenirs de mes soixante ans d'Apostolat*, 17. See also Craig Mishler, "Missionaries in Collision: Anglicans and Oblates among the Gwich'in, 1861–65," *Arctic* 43, no. 2 (1990): 121–26; David W. Leonard, "Anglican and Oblate: The Quest for Souls in the Peace River Country, 1867–1900," *Western Oblate Studies* 3 (1994): 119–38.

70. Séguin to Faraud, Our Lady of Good Hope Mission, February 5, 1874 (Archives Deschâtelets).

71. Séguin to Faraud, Our Lady of Good Hope Mission, February 9, 1877 (Archives Deschâtelets).

72. Séguin to Clut, Fort Good Hope, January 24, 1871, cited in letter from Clut to Fabre, Nativity Mission, May 14, 1871 (Archives Deschâtelets).

73. Séguin to Faraud, Our Lady of Good Hope Mission, July 25, 1870 (Archives Deschâtelets).

74. Séguin to Clut, Fort Good Hope, January 24, 1871, cited in letter from Clut to Fabre, Nativity Mission, May 14, 1871 (Archives Deschâtelets).

75. Séguin to Fabre, Our Lady of Good Hope Mission, May 25, 1871 (OMI General Archives)

76. Séguin to Fabre, Our Lady of Good Hope Mission, May 25, 1871 (OMI General Archives).

77. Séguin to Fabre, Our Lady of Good Hope Mission, May 25, 1871 (OMI General Archives).

78. Séguin to Faraud, Our Lady of Good Hope Mission, July 25, 1870 (Archives Deschâtelets).

79. Séguin to Fabre, Our Lady of Good Hope Mission, May 25, 1871 (OMI General Archives).

80. Séguin to Fabre, Our Lady of Good Hope Mission, June 3, 1874 (OMI General Archives).

81. Pierre Déléage, *Lettres mortes: Essai d'anthropologie inversée* (Paris: Fayard, 2017).

82. On Petitot's later life, see Muller, "L'abbé Émile Petitot," 18–28; Bertrand, "Émile Petitot: Le retour définitif," 65–71.

Bibliography

Works Cited

Abel, Kerry. "Prophets, Priests and Preachers: Dene Shamans and Christian Missions in the Nineteenth Century." *Historical Papers* 21, no. 1 (1986): 211–24.

ben Israel, Menasseh. *The Hope of Israel*. Edited by Henry Méchoulan and Gérard Nahon. Translated by Moses Wall and Richenda George. Oxford: Oxford University Press, 1987 (1650).

Benoit, Dom. *Vie de Mgr Taché*. Vol. 1. Montreal: Librairie Beauchemin, 1904.

Bertrand, Régis. "Émile Petitot (1838–1916) avant ses missions canadiennes: Origine et formation d'un missionnaire oblat." In *La mission et le sauvage: Huguenots et catholiques d'une rive atlantique à l'autre, xvie–xixe*, edited by Nicole Lemaître, 289–303. Paris, Québec: CTHS, Presses de l'Université de Laval, 2008.

———. "Émile Petitot: Le retour définitif en France (1883–1886) et la cure de Mareuil-lès-Meaux (1886–1916)." *Revue d'Histoire et d'Art de la Brie et du Pays de Meaux* 26 (1975): 65–71.

———. "Quelques notes sur les origines, la famille et l'enfance d'Émile Petitot." Unpublished manuscript. Rome, Italy: Archives Générales des Oblats de Marie Immaculée.

Bloch, R. Howard. *Le plagiaire de Dieu*. Paris: Seuil, 1996.

Boltanski, Luc. *Énigmes et complots*. Paris: Gallimard, 2012.

Henry Carnoy. Review of *Accord des mythologies dans la cosmogonie des Danites arctiques*, by Émile Petitot. *La tradition* 5 (1891): 95.

Champagne, Claude. *Les débuts de la mission dans le Nord-Ouest canadien: Mission et Église chez Mgr Vital Grandin, o.m.i., 1829–1902*. Ottawa: Éditions de l'Université Saint-Paul, 1983.

Chapleau, J. A. *Discours de l'Hon. J. A. Chapleau, M. P., sur l'exécution de Louis Riel*. Ottawa: McLean, Roger, 1886.

Choquette, Robert. *The Oblate Assault on Canada's Northwest*. Ottawa: University of Ottawa Press, 1995.

Cooper, David Graham. *The Language of Madness*. London: Penguin Random House, 1980.

De Smet, Pierre-Jean. *Notice sur le territoire et sur la mission de l'Orégon*. Brussels: Bureau de Publication de la Bibliothèque d'Éducation, 1847.

Déléage, Pierre. *Lettres mortes: Essai d'anthropologie inversée*. Paris: Fayard, 2017.

Despine, Prosper. *De la folie au point de vue philosophique ou plus spécialement psychologique étudiée chez le malade et chez l'homme en santé*. Paris: F. Savy, 1875.

Dick, Lyle. "Pibloktoq (Arctic Hysteria): A Construction of European-Inuit Relations?" *Arctic Anthropology* 32, no. 2 (1995): 1–42.

Editor, *Revue critique d'histoire et de littérature: Recueil hebdomadaire* 31, no. 13, (March 30, 1891): n.p.

Francis, Daniel. "A Victorian Scandal: The Asylum at Longue Pointe." *The Beaver* 69, no. 3 (1989): 33–38.

Gagnon, Denis, and Lynn Drapeau. "Les échelles catholiques comme exemples de métissage religieux des ontologies chrétiennes et amérindiennes." *Studies in Religion* 44, no. 2 (2015): 178–207.

Godbey, Allen H. *The Lost Tribes, A Myth: Suggestions towards Rewriting Hebrew History*. Durham, NC: Duke University Press, 1930.

Grandin, Bishop. *Le véritable Riel*. Montreal: Imprimerie générale, 1887.

Grant, John Webster. "Missionaries and Messiahs in the Northwest." *Studies in Religion* 9, no. 2 (1980): 125–36.

Gravier, Gabriel. *L'abbé Petitot chez les grands Esquimaux*. Rouen: Espérance Cagnard, 1888.

Grouard, Émile. "Le R. P. Petitot et le R. P. Grouard au Congrès de Nancy." *Missions de la Congrégation des Missionnaires Oblats de Marie Immaculée* 51 (1875): 397–419.

———. *Souvenirs de mes Soixante ans d'Apostolat dans l'Athabaska-Mackenzie*. Lyon: Œuvres Apostoliques, 1923.

Helm, June. *Prophecy and Power among the Dogrib Indians*. Lincoln: University of Nebraska Press, 1994.

Howard, Henry. "Histoire médicale de Louis David Riel." *L'étendard* (July 13, 1886): 1.

Huddleston, Lee Eldridge. *Origins of the American Indians: European Concepts, 1492–1729*. Austin: University of Texas Press, 1967.

Leonard, David W. "Anglican and Oblate: The Quest for Souls in the Peace River Country, 1867–1900." *Western Oblate Studies* 3 (1994): 119–38.

Mackenzie, Alexander. *Voyages from Montreal, on the River St. Laurence, through the Continent of North America, to the Frozen and Pacific Oceans, in the Years 1789 and 1793*, vol. 1. London: T. Cadell & W. Davies, 1802.

Martel, Gilles. *Le messianisme de Louis Riel*. Waterloo: Wilfrid Laurier University Press, 1984.

Maud, Ralph. *A Guide to B.C. Indian Myth and Legend*. Vancouver: Talonbooks, 1982.

McCarthy, Martha. *From the Great River to the Ends of the Earth: The Missionary Oblates of Mary Immaculate in the Canadian North West*. Edmonton: University of Alberta Press, 1995.

Michel, Fernand. *Dix huit ans chez les sauvages: Voyages et missions de M. Henry Faraud*. Paris: Régis Ruffet, 1866.

Mishler, Craig. "Missionaries in Collision: Anglicans and Oblates among the Gwich'in, 1861–65." *Arctic* 43, no. 2 (1990): 121–26.

Morice, Adrien-Gabriel. *Histoire de l'Église catholique dans l'Ouest canadien, du Lac Supérieur au Pacifique (1659–1905)*, vol. 2. Winnipeg: Chez l'auteur, 1912.

Nagy, Murielle. "Le désir de l'Autre chez le missionnaire Émile Petitot." In *Éros et tabou: Sexualité et genre chez les Amérindiens et les Inuit,* edited by Frédéric Laugrand and Gilles Havard, 408–30. Quebec: Septentrion, 2014.

Paradis, André. "L'asile de 1845 à 1920." In *L'institution médicale,* edited by Normand Séguin, 50–57. Quebec: Presses de l'Université de Laval, 1998.

Petitot, Émile. *Accord des mythologies dans la cosmogonie des Danites arctiques.* Paris: E. Bouillon, 1890.

———. *Autour du Grand lac des Esclaves.* Paris: A. Savine, 1891. (English edition: *Travels around Great Slave and Great Bear Lakes, 1862-1882.* Translated by Paul Laverdure. Toronto: Champlain Society, 2005.)

———. *En route pour la mer glaciale.* Paris: Letouzey & Ané, 1888.

———. "Étude sur la nation montagnaise." *Missions de la Congrégation des Missionnaires Oblats de Marie Immaculée* 24 (1867): 483–547.

———. *Exploration de la région du Grand lac des Ours.* Paris: Téqui, 1893. (English edition: *Travels around Great Slave and Great Bear Lakes, 1862–1882.* Translated by Paul Laverdure. Toronto: Champlain Society, 2005.)

———. "Les Déné-Dindjiés." *Compte-rendu du Congrès international des Américanistes,* vol. 2, 26–37. Nancy: Gustave Crépin-Leblond, 1875.

———. "Les Esquimaux," *Compte rendu du Congrès international des Américanistes,* vol. 1, 329–39. Nancy: Gustave Crépin-Leblond, 1875.

————. *Les grands Esquimaux.* Paris: Plon, 1887. (English edition: *Among the Chiglit Eskimos.* 2nd ed. Translated by E. O. Hahn. Edmonton: University of Alberta Press, Boreal Institute, 1999.)

————. *Origine et migrations des peuples de la Gaule jusqu'à l'avènement des Francs.* Paris: J. Maisonneuve, 1894.

————. *Quinze ans sous le cercle polaire: Mackenzie, Anderson, Youkon.* Paris: E. Dentu, 1889.

————. "Six légendes américaines identifiées à l'histoire de Moïse et du peuple hébreu." *Missions de la Congrégation des Missionnaires Oblats de Marie Immaculée* 60, supplement (1877): 585–751.

————. "Souvenirs de Provence." Unpublished manuscript. Richelieu, Canada: Archives Deschâtelets-Notre-Dame-du-Cap, 1856.

————. "Sur l'habitat et les fluctuations de la population peau rouge, en Canada." *Bulletin et mémoires de la Société d'anthropologie de Paris* 7 (1884): 221–23 (discussion).

————. *Traditions indiennes du Canada Nord-Ouest: Textes originaux et traductions littérales.* Alençon: E. Renaut de Broise, 1887. (English edition: *The Book of Dene: Containing the Traditions and Beliefs of Chipewyan, Dogrib, Slavey, and Loucheux Peoples.* Yellowknife, NWT: Department of Education, Government of the Northwest Territories, 1976.)

————. *Traditions indiennes du Canada Nord-Ouest.* Paris: Maisonneuve, 1886. (English edition: *Indian Legends of North-Western Canada.* Translated by Thelma Habgood. Special Issue: *Athapascan Studies: Western Canadian Journal of Anthropology* 2, no. 2 (1970): 94–129.

Philippe, Victor. "Le Père Émile Petitot et les Esquimaux." Unpublished manuscript attached to letter to Gaston Carrière, Fort Smith (August 20). Richelieu, Canada: Archives Deschâtelets-Notre-Dame-du-Cap, 1983.

Popkin, Richard H. "Jewish Messianism and Christian Millenarianism." In *Culture and Politics from Puritanism to the Enlightenment,* edited by Perez Zagorin, 63–82. Berkeley: University of California Press, 1980.

———. "The Rise and Fall of the Jewish Indian Theory." In *Menasseh ben Israel and his world,* edited by Yosef Kaplan, Henry Méchoulan, and Richard H. Popkin, 63–82. Leiden: Brill, 1989.

Réville, Albert. Review of *Accord des mythologies dans la cosmogonie des Danites arctiques,* by Émile Petitot. *Revue de l'histoire des religions* 22 (1890): 223–24.

Rushforth, Scott. "The Legitimation of Beliefs in a Hunter-Gatherer Society." *American Ethnologist* 19, no. 3 (1992): 483–500.

Saindon, Émile. *En missionnant: Essai sur les missions des Pères Oblats de Marie Immaculée à la Baie James.* Ottawa: Imprimerie du Droit, 1928.

Simons Ronald C., and Charles C. Hughes. *The Culture-Bound Syndromes: Folk Illnesses of Psychiatric and Anthropological Interest.* Dordrecht: D. Rediel, 1985.

Taché, Alexandre. *La situation au Nord-Ouest.* Quebec: J. O. Filteau, 1885.

Taché, Joseph-Charles. *Les asiles d'aliénés de la province de Québec et leurs détracteurs.* Quebec: Hull, 1885.

Tuke, Daniel Hack. *The Insane in the United States and Canada.* London: H. K. Lewis, 1893.

Wauchope, Robert. *Lost Tribes and Sunken Continents: Myth and Method in the Study of American Indians.* Chicago: University of Chicago Press, 1962.

Winchester, Simon. *The Professor and the Madman.* New York: Harper Perennial, 1998.

Correspondence

Most of the letters consulted for this research are unpublished, located in the archives listed below, which also hold the letters published in missionary periodicals.

Archives Deschâtelets-Notre-Dame-du-Cap (Archives Deschâtelets). Richelieu, Canada.

Editor. "Missions d'Amérique." *Annales de la propagation de la foi* 37 (1865): 366–405.

Editors. "Missions du Mackenzie." *Missions de la Congrégation des Missionnaires Oblats de Marie Immaculée* 35 (1870): 270.

General Archives of the Oblates of Mary Immaculate (OMI General Archives). Rome.

Journal of Bishop Grandin, on the Liard River, August 26, 1861. *Missions de la Congrégation des Missionnaires Oblats de Marie Immaculée* 9 (1864): 208–43.

Letter from Hyacinthe Dzanyou, Peau-de-Lièvre des Montagnes Rocheuses, to Petitot, dated February 1874, received in Montreal the following July 24. *Les missions catholiques* 220 (1874): 635. "Athabaska-Mackenzie," *Les missions catholiques* 329 (1875): 463–65.

Letter from Petitot to Fabre, Fort Good Hope, September 15, 1869. *Missions de la Congrégation des Missionnaires Oblats de Marie Immaculée* 35 (1870): 294–310.

Letter from Petitot to Rey, Fort Good Hope, 10 May 1870. *Missions de la Congrégation des Missionnaires Oblats de Marie Immaculée* 36 (1871): 372–75.

Letter from Petitot to Rey, Providence (Mackenzie River rapids), August 18, 1869. *Missions de la Congrégation des Missionnaires Oblats de Marie Immaculée* 35 (1870): 288–94.

Letter from Petitot to the Scholastic brothers and their moderator priest, July 23, 1862. *Missions de la Congrégation des Missionnaires Oblats de Marie Immaculée* 6 (1863): 213–21.

Letter from Petitot, Fort Good Hope, February 29, 1868. *Missions de la Congrégation des Missionnaires Oblats de Marie Immaculée* 31 (1869): 294–310.

Letter from Petitot, Fort Good Hope, July 30, 1869. *Missions de la Congrégation des Missionnaires Oblats de Marie Immaculée* 34 (1870): 186–209.

Letter from Petitot, May 1864. *Missions de la Congrégation des Missionnaires Oblats de Marie Immaculée* 24 (1867): 449–83.

Letter from Petitot, September 1863. *Missions de la Congrégation des Missionnaires Oblats de Marie Immaculé*, 23 (1867): 364–89.

Letter from R. P. Petitot to T. R. P. Superior General. *Missions de la Congrégation des Missionnaires Oblats de Marie Immaculée* 65 (1879): 5–18.

Biographical Works about Émile Petitot

Ballo Alagna, Simonetta. *Émile Petitot: Un capitolo di storia delle esplorazioni Canadesi.* Genoa: Libreria Editrice Mario Bozzi, 1983.

Bertrand, Régis. "Émile Petitot (1838–1916) avant ses missions canadiennes: Origine et formation d'un missionnaire oblat." In *La mission et le sauvage: Huguenots et catholiques d'une rive atlantique à l'autre, xvie–xixe*, edited by Nicole Lemaître, 289–303. Paris, Québec: CTHS, Presses de l'Université de Laval, 2009.

———. "Émile Petitot: Le retour définitif en France (1883–1886) et la cure de Mareuil-lès-Meaux (1886–1916)." *Revue d'Histoire et d'Art de la Brie et du Pays de Meaux* 26 (1975): 65–71.

Cadrin, Gilles. "Émile Petitot, missionnaire dans le Grand Nord canadien: Évangélisateur ou apôtre de la science?" *Mémoires de l'Académie des Sciences, Arts et Belles-lettres de Dijon* 134 (1995): 201–21.

Cerruti, Pietro. "Un problema insoluto della vita del missionario Émile Petitot," *Il Polo* 31, no. 1 (1975): 1–7.

Choquette, Robert. *The Oblate Assault on Canada's Northwest*, 59–66. Ottawa: University of Ottawa Press, 1995.

Déléage, Pierre. "La querelle de 1875." *Recherches amérindiennes au Québec* 45, no. 1 (2015): 39–50.

Haley, Susan. *Petitot: A Novel.* Kentville, NS, Canada: Gatineau Press, 2013.

Laverdure, Paul, Jacqueline R. Moir, and John S. Moir. "Introduction." In *Émile Petitot, Travels around Great Slave and Great Bear Lakes, 1862–1882,* ix–xxxiii. Toronto: Champlain Society, 2005.

Molin, Jean-Baptiste. "Petitot, 'Explorer' and Anthropologist in France," *Bulletin de la Société d'histoire et d'art du Diocèse de Meaux* 24 (1974): 9–17.

Muller, Lambert. "L'abbé Émile Petitot, curé de Mareuil-lès-Meaux." *Bulletin de la Société d'histoire et d'art du Diocèse de Meaux* 24 (1974): 18–28.

Nagy, Murielle. "Devil with the Face of an Angel: Physical and Moral Descriptions of Aboriginal People by Missionary Émile Petitot." In *Indigenous Bodies: Reviewing, Relocating, Reclaiming,* edited by Jacqueline Fear-Segal and Rebecca Tillett, 85–98. Albany: State University of New York Press, 2013.

———. "Le désir de l'Autre chez le missionnaire Émile Petitot." In *Éros et tabou: Sexualité et genre chez les Amérindiens et les Inuit,* edited by Frédéric Laugrand and Gilles Havard, 408–30. Quebec: Septentrion, 2014.

Savoie, Donat. *Les Amérindiens du Nord-Ouest canadien au 19ᵉ siècle selon Émile Petitot.* 2 vols. Ottawa: Bureau des recherches scientifiques sur le Nord, 1970.